Gammer Gurton's Needle

THE NEW MERMAIDS

General Editor: Brian Gibbons
Professor of English Literature, University of Münster

THE NEW MERMAIDS

Gammer Gurton's Needle

Mr. S., Master of Art

Edited by

CHARLES WHITWORTH

Professor of English Renaissance Studies
Centre d'Études et de Recherches sur la Renaissance Anglaise
Université Paul Valéry – Montpellier III
(Associated Unit of the French National Centre for Scientific Research)

LONDON/A & C BLACK

NEW YORK/W W NORTON

For
Tristan Pascal André Charles

Second edition 1997
A & C Black (Publishers) Limited
35 Bedford Row, London WC1R 4JH
ISBN 978-0-7136-4497-5

© *1997 A & C Black (Publishers) Limited*

First New Mermaid edition published 1984
as part of Three Sixteenth-Century Comedies
by Ernest Benn Limited
© *1984 Ernest Benn Limited*

Published in the United States of America by
W. W. Norton & Company Inc.
500 Fifth Avenue, New York, N. Y. 10110

CIP catalogue records for this book
are available from the British Library
and the Library of Congress.

Typeset by Fakenham Photosetting Ltd, Norfolk

CONTENTS

PREFACE TO THE SECOND EDITION

The first New Mermaid edition of *Gammer Gurton's Needle* appeared in *Three Sixteenth-Century Comedies* in 1984. That volume's rather bland title, for which I must accept responsibility, hid two mid-century plays, *Gammer Gurton* and Udall's *Roister Doister*, and Peele's *Old Wife's Tale* from the last decade of the century. The present New Mermaid edition and that of *The Old Wife's Tale* published in 1996 are the fruit of the publisher's and the General Editor's willingness to give some of those plays another chance, each of them on its own this time. I am grateful to them, and especially to Brian Gibbons for his friendly encouragement to undertake the revision, correction and updating necessary to set forth the two elderly ladies, the Old Wife and Gammer Gurton, newly clothed. The 1984 edition recorded the debts of a novice editor to mentors, colleagues, scholars and librarians whose help and encouragement took many forms over many years. Those debts remain outstanding, and others have accumulated in the meantime.

I have profited immeasurably from the work of the Oxford Shakespeare team, led by Professor Stanley Wells, on textual matters: many of the principles which they and others have elaborated and applied to the text of Shakespeare are applicable also to other dramatic texts of the Renaissance. One of the services rendered by series like the New Mermaids is that of submitting texts from the non-Shakespearean dramatic canon to such rigorous re-examination as has been accorded to Shakespeare in the last two decades. Some of the minor readjustments to the 1984 edition made in the present one, concerning stage directions, asides, glosses, and discussions of staging, for example, are indebted to recent Shakespeare scholarship, as well as to the guidelines for New Mermaid editors. Members of the research seminar of the *Centre d'Études et de Recherches sur la Renaissance Anglaise* at Montpellier and of successive *DEA* (pre-doctoral) seminars have repeatedly challenged my thinking about the business of editing early texts, as well as in larger domains such as ways of recovering English medieval and Tudor culture for modern students and readers, including non-English speaking ones. I am particularly grateful to Jean-Marie Maguin for personal and professional support, innumerable profitable conversations, and scholarly advice on country matters, as well as his illuminating pages on the nocturnal setting of the play.

The depth and breadth of the knowledge of French scholars of English drama never cease to inspire admiration. I have learned much from the work of colleagues in France, some of them specialists in early Tudor drama: if I mention Jean-Paul Debax, and André Lascombes and the excellent *tables rondes* on Tudor drama at Tours in which I was honoured to participate in 1991 and 1995,

I trust that other friends and colleagues will not take umbrage at
not being named here. Those events at Tours have also provided
welcome opportunities to learn anew from Peter Happé and
Richard and Marie Axton among other distinguished scholars of
early English drama. In the last few years, they and others have
helped keep me in touch with the age which produced *Gammer
Gurton's Needle*.

I have rewritten the introduction, and rechecked and corrected
the text for this new edition; there were relatively few substantive
errors in the first, for which thanks are due to its proofreaders and
printers. I have modified punctuation, which I think was too heavy,
and stage directions; in the latter case, I have benefited from some
of William Tydeman's suggestions in his *Four Tudor Comedies*, an
old-spelling edition published in 1984, at the same time as *Three
Sixteenth-Century Comedies*. The 'Further Reading' list has been ex-
panded and updated. Significant new publications on the play are
few and far between; I have tried to provide a substantial, wide-
ranging but still selective bibliography. Inevitably, errors and short-
comings remain, even in a revised edition, and just as inevitably,
prefaces are the occasions for owning up to them.

Montpellier, August 1996   C.W.W.

ABBREVIATIONS

I. *Texts; editions collated and cited*

Q	1575 quarto of *Gammer Gurton's Needle*
1661	Reprint of 1575 quarto
Adams	Joseph Quincy Adams, ed., *Chief Pre-Shakespearean Dramas* (1924)
Baskervill, et al.	C. R. Baskervill, V. B. Heltzel, A. H. Nethercot, eds., *Elizabethan and Stuart Plays* (New York, 1934)
Boas	F. S. Boas, ed., *Five Pre-Shakespearean Comedies* (1934; repr. 1970)
Bradley	Henry Bradley, ed., *Gammer Gurton's Needle*, in Gayley
Brett-Smith	H. F. B. Brett-Smith, ed., *Gammer Gurton's Needle*, Percy Reprints (Oxford, 1920)
Creeth	Edmund Creeth, ed., *Tudor Plays* (New York, 1966)
Gayley	Charles Mills Gayley, ed., *Representative English Comedies* (1903)

Hazlitt	W. Carew Hazlitt, ed., *A Select Collection of Old English Plays*, fourth edition, 15 vols (1874–76), III
Manly	J. M. Manly, ed., *Specimens of the Pre-Shakespearean Drama*, 2 vols (Boston, 1897), II
Tydeman	William Tydeman, ed., *Four Tudor Comedies* (Harmondsworth, 1984)

II. *Reference works*

EES	Glynne Wickham, *Early English Stages 1300–1660*, 3 vols (1959–81)
ODEP	*The Oxford Dictionary of English Proverbs*, compiled by William George Smith, third edition, ed. F. P. Wilson (Oxford, 1970)
OED	*Oxford English Dictionary*
REED	Records of Early English Drama
Southern	Richard Southern, *The Staging of Plays before Shakespeare* (1973)
Tilley	Morris Palmer Tilley, *A Dictionary of the Proverbs in England in the Sixteenth and Seventeenth Centuries* (Ann Arbor, Michigan, 1950)

III. *Periodicals and series*

ELN	*English Language Notes*
MSC	Malone Society Collections
N&Q	*Notes and Queries*
Ren D	*Renaissance Drama*
SEL	*Studies in English Literature 1500–1900*

IV. *Other abbreviations*

ed.	this edition	eds	other editions
Fr.	French	L.	Latin
s.d.	stage direction	s.p.	speech prefix

Works of classical authors are cited in the Loeb Classical Library editions, Shakespeare in the Oxford Shakespeare *Complete Works*, ed. Stanley Wells and Gary Taylor (1986), other dramatists in the New Mermaid editions, unless otherwise indicated. Place of publication is London, unless otherwise indicated.

INTRODUCTION

BACKGROUND

> The more we study Shakespeare ... the more we perceive that his pre-
> decessors, no less than his successors, exist for him. ... Having him, we could
> well dispense with them.[1]

These words were written a century ago, and reflect the evolutionary ideology that permeated virtually all fields of scholarly endeav-
our. The language of Darwinian theory and scienticism is to be
found in countless essays and introductions to collections of
English plays, even in titles: 'specimen', 'species', 'evolution', 'per-
mutation', 'genus'. The study of literature was 'literary science', a
text was a 'specimen', a genre a 'genus'. The great E. K. Chambers,
whose work on early drama remains a watershed in the history of
literary scholarship, apologized for his failure to reach an 'austere
standard of scientific completeness'.[2] Symonds, in the passage
quoted above, merely states in bald form the prevailing view of the
utility of studying pre-Shakespearean drama; for him and his contemporaries, such study was the necessary preliminary to the full
appreciation of their ultimate object of devotion, the works of
Shakespeare. This teleological view was implicit in major studies of
early drama well into the middle of the twentieth century.[3]

As one approached the Elizabethan age from the allegedly bleak
landscape that stretched back from the Shakespearean promontory
across the centuries to the primitive beginnings in liturgical tropes
and Latin church drama, a few oases were perceptible. The early
Tudor period appeared particularly rich in remains. A. P. Rossiter
seems almost to parody the evolutionists' imagery:

> From the reign of Henry VIII (1509-47) to that of Elizabeth, the dramatic
> world is like a seething primordial swamp in which local time is, so to speak,
> accelerated, and a confused wealth of forms emerge, few of which last long.[4]

---

[1] John Addington Symonds, *Shakespere's Predecessors in the English Drama* (1900), pp.
14-15.

[2] *The Medieval Stage*, 2 vols (1903), I, viii. An influential collection was J. M. Manly's
Specimens of the Pre-Shakespearean Drama, 2 vols (Boston, 1897).

[3] For example, in Hardin Craig's *English Religious Drama of the Middle Ages* (Oxford,
1955). The most succinct résumé and acute critique of the evolutionary approach to
early drama remains the first essay in O. B. Hardison's *Christian Rite and Christian
Drama in the Middle Ages* (Baltimore, 1965), pp. 1-34.

[4] *English Drama from Early Times to the Elizabethans* (1950), p. 108.

By the mid-sixteenth century, both native forms – the Corpus Christi and Whitsun cycles, morality plays, saint plays, various kinds of secular interludes and folk drama – and classical exemplars, notably Terence and Plautus, familiar from the school curriculum, had been absorbed and commingled. Anonymous clerical playwrights, Protestant and Catholic propagandists, Humanist scholars, university dons, and schoolmasters all contributed to that 'seething swamp' of dramatic activity that marks the decades from the 1520s to the 1560s. It is in the early Tudor period that the first important named English dramatists can be identified: Medwall, Rastell, Skelton, Heywood, Redford, Udall, Bale.

Among the welter of emerging forms, comedy was a particularly hardy genus. The Roman dramatist Terence had never been absent from the school curriculum throughout the Middle Ages; schoolmasters felt his comedies to be more edifying than those of Plautus and his Latin more eloquent and worthy of emulation. As early as the tenth century the German nun Hrotsvitha had written Latin plays explicitly modelled on those of Terence. The earliest Renaissance printed texts were accompanied by the commentaries of Donatus, a fourth-century grammarian, whose precepts on comic structure, derived from Terence's practice, had the same authority as that enjoyed in the later Renaissance by Aristotle's *Poetics* with respect to tragedy.[5] The importance of Terence in the early sixteenth century can scarcely be understated. Erasmus and the German Reformer Melanchthon, among others, wrote commentaries on his comedies. The first, anonymous, English translations of a play by Terence, *Andria*, dates from around 1530.[6] In 1534, a major English dramatist, the humanist scholar and educator Nicholas Udall, published *Flowers for Latin Speaking Selected and Gathered out of Terence*, demonstrating the centrality of the Roman playwright in the Humanists' educational programme. Udall's best play, *Roister Doister* (c. 1552) exemplifies the classical structure and borrows from both Terence's *Eunuchus* and Plautus's *Miles Gloriosus*.[7]

But English dramatists had other, native, models as well. Folk plays, pageants, and farces had existed for centuries. The fragmentary farcical *Interludium de Clerico et Puella* dates from the thirteenth

---

[5] On the influence of Terence and Plautus in the period, see T. W. Baldwin, *William Shakespere's Five-Act Structure* (Urbana, Illinois, 1947), and on that of Donatus, Marvin T. Herrick, *Comic Theory in the Sixteenth Century* (Urbana, Illinois, 1950; repr. 1964).

[6] See the edition by Meg Twycross, *Terence in English: That Girl from Andros* (Lancaster, 1987).

[7] On Udall, see C. W. Whitworth, ed., *Three Sixteenth-Century Comedies* (1984), pp. xxxiv–xxxvii.

century.[8] The epic Corpus Christi cycles which flourished in cities
and large towns from the late fourteenth century were rich in comic
characters and techniques. The very form of religious drama, de-
picting Christ's triumph over Satan, with its promise of redemption
and eternal life for sinful mortals, was comic: the divine comedy.
Morality and saint plays and interludes, moral and secular, were
famous for their devils, vices, villains, braggarts and dupes. If the
devil and human vice, which came to be personified as the Vice
(first named as such by John Heywood), were ultimately to be van-
quished, one could in all good conscience enjoy their skulduggery,
bluster and blasphemy in the meantime. Dramatists were quick to
exploit that natural tension between moral consciousness and basic
human nature. Shakespeare's Richard of Gloucester, Iago and
Falstaff, Marlowe's Barabas, Jonson's Face and Mosca, Webster's
Flamineo and a host of others are, in part, the descendants of characters like Mak in the Wakefield *Second Shepherds' Play*, and of gen-
erations of Vices called Mischief, Idleness, Iniquity and the like. So
too, in part, is Diccon of Bedlam.

AUTHORSHIP AND DATE

Few sixteenth-century title-pages can have posed such troublesome
questions as this one: 'A Ryght/Pithy, Pleasaunt and me-/rie
Comedie: In-/tytuled *Gammer gur-/tons Nedle*: Played on/Stage, not
longe/ ago in Chri-/stes/ *Colledge in Cambridge*. Made by Mr. S. Mr
of Art'.[9] There is no date, but that omission is remedied in the
printer's colophon on the last page of the quarto: 'Imprinted at
London/ in Fleetstreate beneath the Conduite,/ at the signe of S.
John Evangelist,/ by/ Thomas Colwell./ 1575'. For more than two
hundred years, educated guesses have been made as to the identity
of 'Mr. S.', and at least one explicit attribution of the play to a
known author was made in the sixteenth century. Stage historians
have been intrigued by the statement that the play was 'played on
stage'. This is the earliest extant work for which that explicit claim
is made.

The questions and puzzles do not stop there. The publication
date is 1575, and the quarto of that year (Q) is the only sixteenth-
century edition, but there was an entry in the Stationers' Register

---

[8] Glynne Wickham gives parallel texts in *English Moral Interludes* (1976), pp. 199–
203. He cites the *Interludium* as 'making nonsense of the idea, current for so long
among critics and historians, that religious drama had to be "secularized" before art
of any merit in dramatic form could develop' (p. 196).
[9] On the title-page reproduction in this edition, 'and' is misprinted 'anp'. See section
on 'This Edition' below.

for the year 1562–3, licensing Thomas Colwell to print a play called *Dyccon of Bedlam*. Diccon is a principal character in *Gammer Gurton's Needle*, Colwell is the printer, and the coincidence seems too great to be only that. On the title-page of Q, the words '*Gammer gurtons Nedle*' are printed in a different type, italic, from the black-letter of the surrounding lines; the type size is also smaller, as if to cram more letters into the available space. This indeed was the suggestion made by Henry Bradley, an early modern editor of the play: he thought that the title had been altered from *Dyccon of Bedlam* to *Gammer Gurtons Nedle*, and the typeface and size accordingly changed to fit the slightly longer title into the available space on a title-page that had already been set up.[10] But would a title-page printed in 1563 be held in the printer's shop for twelve years pending publication of the play? And what does 'not long ago' mean? 'Not long ago' from when? May there have been editions of the play, under either title, before 1575? If so no traces of them remain, yet Q survives in eleven copies, an exceptionally high number for the kind of ephemeral publication that play texts were. The next known edition, that of 1661, was printed directly from a copy of Q, and preserves most of its numerous errors.

The mystery of the play's authorship has provoked more speculation than that of its date, though the two mysteries are closely related. With only the initial 'S' for guidance, and armed with the title-page's claim that it was played at Christ's College, Cambridge (though not that it was *written* by a member of that college), scholars have sought for a member of Christ's whose surname begins with 'S' and who was known to be involved in college dramatic activities at a time corresponding to 'not long' before the 1562–3 Stationers' Register entry of what is assumed to be the same play, assuming further that that date and not 1575 is the point of departure for the 'not long ago' reference. John Peile, compiling a history of the college, found in the bursar's accounts for 1550–1, 1551–2, and 1553–4 records for payments to a certain 'Sir Stephenson' for plays.[11] Henry Bradley found a further reference to 'Mr

[10] Bradley's edition is in Gayley, pp. 195–261; the theory about the printing of the title-page is on p. 199. The only other extant play printed by Colwell, William Ingelend's *The Disobedient Child* (c. 1560), has the title in uniform type, but also lacks the date.

[11] John Peile, *Christ's College*, University of Cambridge College Histories (1990), p. 54. The 1553–4 entry reads 'Expended by Mr. Stephenson at setting furth of his plaie ...'; Stevenson received his M.A. in 1553. 'The Academic Drama at Cambridge: Extracts from College Records' was edited by G. C. Moore Smith in MSC, II, pt. 2 (1923). More recently, Alan H. Nelson has edited all available documents in his monumental *Cambridge* in the Records of Early English Drama, 2 vols (Toronto, 1989); see esp. pp. 167, 173, 184–5, 748–9, 897–8. Nelson also notes another payment to Stevenson, for music, in 1549–50.

Stevenson's play' in the 1559–60 accounts. Bradley concluded reasonably that 'Mr. S.', author of *Gammer Gurton's Needle*, was the Stevenson involved in the production of plays at Christ's College in the 1550s. There was indeed a William Stevenson who was a Fellow of Christ's, as Bachelor of Arts (hence the title 'Sir', i.e., *dominus*) from 1550 to 1553, and again as Master of Arts ('Mr') in 1559–60. He disappears from the dramatic records (after Christmas 1553) and from the list of Fellows (after March 1554) in the interim. Those years coincide exactly with the reign of Mary Tudor, when Protestant Reformers were being persecuted. A number of Cambridge men were among the Marian exiles in Europe. Christ's College was strongly Edwardian in its sympathies, and later became positively Puritan; the Master, Richard Wilkes, was ejected in 1553. Very possibly, Stevenson found it prudent to leave with others, and returned only in 1559, after the accession of Elizabeth and the end of the persecutions. He soon left the university for good, however, having become Bachelor of Divinity in 1560. He was named to a prebend in Durham Cathedral in 1561, and his death is recorded in 1575, the year the play was published.

Stevenson certainly seems the most likely candidate for the authorship of *Gammer Gurton's Needle*. The circumstantial evidence is strong. It may be noted however that the Christ's College records do not specify that Stevenson *wrote* plays, only that he was remunerated for his disbursements incurred in 'setting forth', that is, producing them. Nor, unfortunately, do the Christ's records name plays. Some other colleges' accounts do; many entries take the form of those in the Trinity College records: 'Item paid to Mr Legge for ye expenses abought the setting forthe of *Medea*', or 'to Master Shaclocke for the charges of *pseudolus*' (MSC, II.2, pp. 161, 163). The plays named are Roman plays, by Seneca and Plautus respectively, and Legge and Shacklock produced them. There are occasional references to unnamed 'English Plays', and those may have been written as well as produced by members of the colleges. The 1553–4 entry in the Christ's accounts records payments to Stevenson for 'setting furth of his plaie', and to Mr. Perceval 'at ye latten plaie'; perhaps the distinction means that 'his plaie' was Stevenson's own composition (Nelson, REED, p. 184). If *Gammer Gurton's Needle* is one of the plays mentioned in connection with Stevenson's name in the Christ's accounts, it must have been written and produced either between 1550 and 1553, or in 1559–60. The phrase 'in the king's name' in the play (V.ii.234), if taken to refer to the state of the monarchy in England, would indicate a date of composition not later than mid-1553, when Edward VI died. On the other hand, a span of ten years or more does not sound like 'not long ago', while 1559–60 would be, relatively, not long before 1562–3 – assuming that the title-page information dates from the year of the S.R. entry. But 'in the king's name' may be no more than authorial license; this is fiction, after all, and its world need not correspond in every detail to the real state of affairs in England at the time. There is little or no topical allusion in the play, so dating from internal evidence is not possible.

Before Stevenson was nominated by Bradley, two other candidates had been proposed. One, John Still, Bishop of Bath and Wells, was suggested by Isaac Reed in 1782, and disposed of by C. H. Ross in 1897; nevertheless, some library catalogues still enter the play under Still's name.[12] Stevenson's main rival is John Bridges, Dean of Salisbury Cathedral, later Bishop of Oxford, who left several theological treatises and translations. Against Bridges are the facts that he was not a Christ's College, but rather a Pembroke Hall man, and that his name, obviously, does not begin with 'S'. It ends in 's', however, and it has been argued, perhaps too cleverly, that the title-page attribution to 'Mr. S.' was a deliberate decoy to protect the author's anonymity.[13] The chief evidence for Bridges's authorship of the play comes in the attribution made by 'Martin Marprelate', pseudonymous author of a series of virulent Puritan pamphlets of the late 1580s attacking the Anglican episcopate and hierarchy, of which Bridges was already a highly visible member. These pamphlets and the equally virulent (and scurrilous) rejoinders from the Anglican side, written by literary men hired for the purpose, including John Lyly and Thomas Nashe, constitute the notorious 'Marprelate Controversy'.

Bridges was one of the prelates marred by Martin. He was by then Dean of Salisbury and had written forcefully in defence of the Anglican cause against both Puritan and Catholic opponents. His vigorous *Defence of the Government Established in the Church of England for Ecclesiastical Matters*, published in 1587, attracted the wrath of Martin. In 'The Epistle', published in October 1588, Martin (possibly John Penry, who had written anti-episcopal tracts in his own name) addresses Bridges:

> You have been a worthy writer, as they say, of a long time; your first book was a proper interlude, called *Gammer Gurton's Needle*. But I think that this trifle, which showeth the author to have had some wit and invention in him, was none of your doing, because your books seem to proceed from the brains of a woodcock, as having neither wit nor learning.
>
> (Boas, *University Drama*, p. 83, spelling modernized)

This is scarcely an unambiguous ascription. Is emphasis to be put

[12] C. H. Ross, 'The Authorship of *Gammer Gurton's Needle*', *Anglia*, 19 (1897), 306–11.

[13] Joseph Hunter, quoted by F. S. Boas, *University Drama in the Tudor Age* (Oxford, 1914), p. 84. Boas, like Ross, argues for Bridges's authorship.

upon the explicit statement 'your first book was ... *Gammer Gurton's Needle*', or upon Martin's claim to disbelieve that Bridges was capable of the 'wit and invention' evinced in the play? (It is curious enough that the arch-Puritan should allow that a play, and such a 'trifle' as this, might boast these admirable literary qualities). However we may choose to answer that, it is hard to see why Martin would allege – whether to confirm or to deny – Bridges's authorship of the play thirteen years after the publication of the only quarto, and thirty years or more after its likely date of composition, if there were nothing whatsoever in the charge. But it is not simply an isolated shot in the dark, as two further allusions, in the sequel to 'The Epistle', make clear. In 'The Epitome', published just a month later, and likewise addressed to Bridges, Martin renews the charge: 'Let me take you again in such a prank, and I'll course you, as you were better to be seeking Gammer Gurton's needle, than come within my fingers' (Boas, *University Drama*, p. 84). Later, Martin rebukes Bridges for asserting something without citing an authority, and asks him where he found it: 'What if he found it in Hodge's breeches, seeking for Gammer Gurton's needle?'

It is difficult to imagine why Martin should invent Bridges's authorship of the play out of whole cloth. Even if that were credible as an interpretation of the first passage – he wished to damage the Dean's reputation by accusing him of writing a notoriously coarse, decidedly unchurchman-like play, or he pretended to have heard it said that Bridges wrote a play famous for its wit, only to be able to declare it beyond the capacity of someone with the 'brains of a woodcock' – he would, it seems, have had little reason to continue to insist upon the fabrication in his next pamphlet. The insult would have lost its shock value. Perhaps then Bridges's name was associated in some way with the play, even if only in university and ecclesiastical circles, the main readership of the Marprelate tracts. Martin hoped to score points and embarrass his adversary by reminding readers of the learned dean's less staid, more frivolous past as a young Cambridge don, however many years ago that past now was. Or Martin may have been entirely mistaken and his hearsay evidence unfounded. But John Penry, probable author of 'The Epistle' and 'The Epitome', had been supplied with slanderous material on important churchmen by those who engaged him to write his attacks. His sources may well have discovered that Bridges had had something to do with the play in some capacity years before. If not, why bother to invent it? Other, more pointed and damaging accusations could presumably have been made. At any rate, neither Bridges nor anyone else seems to have bothered to refute the charge.

Boas argues that Bridges might well have had his play performed at Christ's or elsewhere if his own college, Pembroke Hall, did little or nothing in that vein. Richard Legge, when master of Gonville and Caius College, had his Latin play, *Richardus Tertius*, performed at St. John's. Pembroke is not among the colleges for which dramatic records from the mid-sixteenth century survive. Bridges took his B.A. in 1556, his M.A. in 1560. 'Mr. of Art' and 'not long ago', if the title-page dates from 1562-3 at the latest, would make sense if they referred to Bridges and to performance of the play at Christ's within the preceding two or three years. So Bridges, like Stevenson, was at Cambridge at the right time, or one of the possibly right times (c. 1553-60), and he did write, at least he wrote later in his career; we have no hard evidence that the 'Mr. Stevenson' who was a fellow of Christ's and who was paid for 'setting forth' plays did write. The stumbling block is Martin Marprelate's credibility as a witness and the dubious nature of the document in which he asserts Bridges's authorship of our play.

No one, I believe, has taken up Bradley's passing suggestion that Bridges may have revised Stevenson's earlier work, possibly for a revival in the early 1560s (Gayley, p. 200). Whether revision, collaboration, or a case of Stevenson the producer staging Bridges the author's play, *Gammer Gurton's Needle* may have been touched by both men. If both were involved in its early Cambridge history in some way, it would be plausible for its publication, planned for 1562-3, to be postponed in deference to the reputations of both: both were churchmen by then. When it was finally published in 1575, the year of Stevenson's death, Bridges was already such a prominent figure in his profession that he would scarcely have acknowledged his paternity; it was simply published without his express approval. If it was Stevenson's, and had remained unprinted for years following its creation, its appearance in the very year of his death, may be just coincidence, another tantalizing bit of a jigsaw puzzle many of whose key pieces remain lost. Or, its author dead, a tacit statute of limitations was deemed to have lapsed, and Colwell was at last free to make what profit he could from the 'trifle' whose reputation now extended well beyond the college walls.

F. P. Wilson remarked with reference to another excellent anonymous play of the period, *Respublica*: 'There is a natural reluctance to allow a work that stands above the ruck to remain anonymous. We do not like to see valuables lying about unattached'.[14] To sum up: despite our desire to father so lively a child on a named person, the evidence either way is simply not conclusive. Stevenson has be-

---

[14] *The English Drama 1485-1585*, Oxford History of English Literature (1969), p. 42.

come the acknowledged author by common assent on strong circumstantial evidence, though there is no proof that he ever wrote anything at all. His name begins with 'S', he appears several times in the Christ's College dramatic records between three and thirteen years prior to the entry of a play entitled *Diccon of Bedlam* in the Stationers' Register: these facts constitute his claim to the authorship of *Gammer Gurton's Needle*. John Bridges, a prolific writer, who was also at Cambridge at the right time is named explicitly as author of the play by a contemporary witness whose motive may certainly be suspect but who reiterates his claim, while Bridges appears not to have denied the attribution. But 'S' is the wrong letter and Christ's the wrong college. I believe that until further evidence comes to light, we can only continue to attribute the play to 'Mr.S., Master of Art'. 'S' may after all stand only for 'Somebody'.[15]

This major uncertainty leaves the date of the play uncertain as well, with 1550–3 and 1559–62 both possible; Stevenson's candidacy fits either period, Bridges's probably only the latter. The latter seems more likely if 'not long ago' on the title-page is allowed significance (though it might refer to revivals of an older play still in the college's possession). But if 'in the king's name' is taken to refer to the actual English monarch at the time the play was written, the earlier span of years is forced upon us: no king reigned in England for fifty years after July 1553. The play's glib irreverence towards saints, oaths and relics, and the unmistakable satirical relish with which the parish clergy is caricatured in the person of the pompous, dim-witted, bibulous Doctor Rat the curate, make Mary's reign (mid-1553–8) seem rather less likely than the latter years of her half-brother Edward's, or possibly the first years of her half-sister Elizabeth's. The weight of evidence would seem to be in favour of the earlier years of the decade: *Gammer Gurton's Needle* is probably neither a Marian nor an Elizabethan play, but, like its rival for the title of 'first English regular comedy', Udall's *Roister Doister,* an Edwardian one.

CONVENTIONS AND GENRE

Martin Marprelate was right at least about the author's 'wit and in-

[15] In a note in the 1984 New Mermaid edition, I inclined very hesitantly towards Bridges, partly to be cantankerous and register scepticism toward the growing consensus in favour of Stevenson. I still find the insistent Marprelate claims puzzling if there is no glimmer of factual basis to them, but, encouraged by Nelson's research and the cumulative weight of the circumstantial evidence, I would lean the other way now. I prefer though the safety and the enigma of 'Mr. S.' I make no apology for reviewing the authorship problem thoroughly in this, the first separate critical edition of the play in nearly eighty years.

vention', whoever he may have been. It is a *tour de force*, the extremely clever, spirited, outrageous production of an inventive, gifted dramatist and humorist. It is university students' entertainment, no doubt performed during some such time of seasonal merry-making as the Christmas holidays when the Lord of Misrule, or Christmas Lord, presided over feasts and frolics. Such festivals of hierarchical inversion and licensed anarchy survived in universities and Inns of Court long after the church had suppressed them (*EES*, III, 84). The play is a dramatic embodiment of carnival, as Bakhtin describes it in his classic study: earthy, violent, vulgar, anarchic, all belly, bowels and blows.[16] A rare example of a university play in the vernacular, *Gammer Gurton's Needle* is pure low comedy, farce, devoid of even the moderately corrective bias of Roman comedy, let alone the spiritual and moral gravity of the moralities. In this respect, it is untypical of the majority of comedies of the period, including its contemporary, Udall's *Roister Doister*, which retain something of the admired Terentian decorum if not the moral plays' outright didacticism. To a greater extent than any other play of its time, its sole aim is to delight. Much of the delight for its original audience derived, of course, from their familiarity with the dramatic and literary prototypes that it imitates, adapts and parodies.

Mr. S., a university don, obviously knew the comedies of Terence and Plautus. His adoption of their five-act structure for his native, vernacular and extremely homely matter is part of the joke. The 'homely world of village japes and jealousies' recalls the lolling, belching local tavern society of Langland's *Piers Plowman*, Chaucer's hectic barnyard in the *Nun's Priest's Tale*, the domestic brawling of John Lydgate's *Mummimg at Hertford* in the early fifteenth century, the boozy riot and name-calling of Skelton's *Tunning of Elinor Rumming*, the wicked humour of John Heywood's farces of the early 1530s. The play's most interesting character, Diccon, exhibits the variety of influences and dramatic traditions which converge in the play. Though called 'the Bedlam', that is a former inmate of St. Mary of Bethlehem Hospital in London, an insane asylum, he is far from mad. Indeed he has more wits than anyone else except possibly Master Bailey, who methodically and calmly sorts out the web of misunderstandings and misrepresentations woven by Diccon. He lives by his wits, as he gleefully informs us in I.i.1–6, 22–4. He may be a beggar, wandering from place to place, but he is clearly known to the villagers (II.ii.22; II.iv.7; V.ii.151–3). He arrives in the midst of a domestic drama: Gammer Gurton has lost her only needle, Hodge her man desperately needs

[16] Mikhail Bakhtin, *Rabelais and His World*, trans. Hélène Iswolsky (Bloomington, Indiana, 1984; original Russian edition, 1965).

his other pair of trousers mended, the household, down to Gib the cat, is in an uproar. Diccon seizes the occasion to compound the chaos. In the farcical context of this play's world, Diccon is mischievous, no worse, but he owes as much to the Vices of the English moralities and interludes and the raucous servants of the Corpus Christi cycles (e.g., Pikeharness in the Wakefield *Killing of Abel*) as to the scheming, mocking pages and valets of Roman comedy (such as Davus in Terence's *Andria*). He sows dissension 'for sport' by the simple expedients of lying and insinuating, playing upon the gullibility or credulity of his victims, then denies everything. He is like the fox in the episode from the Reynard cycle printed in the Appendix, leading his victim into a trap by enticement. He is also the presenter, master of ceremonies, solicitous of his audience's enjoyment and comfort, calling for music between the acts. He straddles the boundary between play world and audience, turning to the latter to confide and prepare them for his next prank, returning to the play to perform his catalytic role as troublemaker, with a wink over his shoulder and a promise of more 'sport' in the offing. He speaks the brief epilogue.[17] Prior to *Gammer Gurton's Needle*, few characters in English secular drama demonstrate the rich mixture of conventions or move with such ease between play and audience. Only the ubiquitous servants A and B in Medwall's splendid early comedy *Fulgens and Lucres* (c. 1497) are truly comparable. It too is a hall play, and the features of that kind of theatre, conducive to the blurring of boundaries, will be discussed under 'Staging' below.

When Diccon, by his barefaced lies, has set Dame Chat and Gammer Gurton at odds, he clears off to let the mischief work, promising his audience rare sport if once the two incensed dames should meet (II.v). Their titanic battle, inspired by French farce and *fabliau* via such native examples as Heywood's *The Pardoner and the Friar*, is the play's centrepiece (III.iii). As Wickham notes, it is the first stage fight in English drama between two pantomime dames (*EES*, III, 88). Not yet satisfied, Diccon lures Doctor Rat, the curate, into a trap set at Diccon's instigation by Dame Chat to catch a chicken thief whom she supposes to be her neighbour's farm labourer Hodge. Thus new characters, new intrigue and more farcical knockabout are introduced in Act IV. The final act brings in Master Bailey, the bailiff, and his silent catchpole Scapethrift, and the last scene, the play's longest, sees finally the untangling of Diccon's well-spun web and the recovery of the needle, where it had been since the beginning.

---

[17] In a 1982 touring production by the Medieval Players, Diccon also spoke the Prologue, which was accompanied by a dumbshow, then went straight into his own speech in I.i.

The construction is masterly, the work of a scholar well versed in classical drama and theory; the humour is full-blooded and thoroughly English. Its language is vivid, racy, laced with proverbs and folk wisdom, extravagant oaths, and colloquialisms. The dramatist distinguishes carefully between the members of Gammer Gurton's household – Gammer herself, Hodge, Tib, Cock – who speak the rustic stage dialect, already conventional by this time, marked by 'ich' (for 'I') and the elided 'ch-' form, and the other characters who do not: Diccon, Chat, Rat, Bailey. A number of words and expressions have their first recorded occurrence in this play. The verse is rhymed couplets of the long variety which predominates in dramatic writing in the period between the early sixteenth century, when stanzaic verse still prevailed, and the later decades of the century, when blank verse began to assert itself as the natural medium for drama. The irregular long lines, sometimes fourteeners, sometimes hexameters, often not readily scannable as either, prove remarkably flexible in the hands of the Cambridge dramatist, their natural heaviness, often wearisome in non-dramatic verse or in a more formal dramatic style, offset by the verve of the language. It is abundantly clear that live drama for performance rather than dramatic poetry for reading was Mr. S.'s objective. He sometimes varies the long, 'tumbling' line, as when Hodge and Diccon speak in six-line tail-rhyme stanzas (II.i.71–end), continued by Diccon in the first speech of II.ii, and when Doctor Rat speaks mainly four-stress lines at the end of IV.iv. The drinking song in Act II and instrumental interludes provided further variety for the play's first audiences in the hall of Christ's College in the 1550s.

AFTERLIFE

For a university play, with such an obscure early history, *Gammer Gurton's Needle* became remarkably well known, almost a by-word in literary and theatrical circles, despite apparently not having been printed for more than twenty years after its composition and earliest performance. Besides the allusions by Martin Marprelate, already discussed, whatever their significance may be, there are also echoes in other plays of the period. References to Gib the cat and to Hob Filcher's (apparently an alehouse) are found in Ulpian Fulwell's *Like Will to Like* (1568), which also contains a drinking song reminiscent of the one in *Gammer Gurton's Needle*. The forty-line seventh scene of Francis Merbury's *The Marriage Between Wit and Wisdom* (1579) is modelled closely in both its coarse language and its rambunctious action on *Gammer Gurton's Needle*: the servants Doll and Lob are beaten by their mistress, Mother Bee, for allowing a pottage-pot to be stolen while they were 'tumbling' in the barn, Lob has a torn trouser breech, Inquisition brings in the Vice Idleness who has taken the pot and who claims to be able to tell who has stolen the 'cock with the yellow legs', etc.[18] The scene is entirely gratuitous, and Merbury clearly stuck it in to capitalize on the popularity of such low-comic episodes; his main morality action derives from an earlier play by John Redford, *Wit and Science*. In the 1599 satirical comedy *Histriomastix*, there is a reference to '*Mother Gurton's Needle*, a tragedy' in the repertory of Sir Oliver Owlet's men.[19] Even such fame in the decades immediately following its publication does not account, however, for the unexpected appearance of a new edition in 1661, the year after the Restoration of Charles II and a century or more after its composition, when it must have seemed quaint, to say the least. New private theatres had just opened in Lincoln's Inn Fields and Bridges Street, and new companies, the King's and the Duke's, with the first actresses to perform on the English stage, played in them; authors like Cowley, Davenant, and the Howards were supplying them with the first Restoration plays. Another dramatist and one of the publishers of the 1661 *Gammer Gurton's Needle* was Francis Kirkman (1632– c. 1681), author of *The Wits*, a bookseller and collector of old plays. It is most likely his antiquarian enthusiasm that was responsible for the reprint, and probably his own copy of the 1575 quarto that provided the text.

Gammer Gurton's Needle has not always been so popular or well regarded. Its obvious merits as high-spirited entertainment have been lost on some critics who could see little but crude language and excessive scatology. Its first modern editor, Bradley, sniffed at 'the very rudimentary kind of humour which turns on physically disgusting suggestions no longer amusing to educated people'. There was far too much of 'this poor stuff' for Bradley's late-Victorian taste, though he did discern 'real comedy, not quite of the lowest order' in some scenes (Gayley, pp. 202–3).[20] Educated Victorians may not have been amused (or may not have shown it if they were). But we should not suppose, as patronizing critics used to do, that educated Elizabethans were capable of appreciating only that 'very rudimentary kind of humour'. The play's excrementiousness is a vital aspect of its carnival mood. It is college men's up-

[18] Wickham, ed., *English Moral Interludes*, pp. 188–9.
[19] Quoted in M. C. Bradbrook, *The Growth and Structure of Elizabethan Comedy* (1955), p. 41.
[20] Compare another early twentieth-century editor, Brett-Smith: 'Scholarly persons, living in academic celibacy, have often a singular taste for the matters of low life, and find in the crude humour and gross speech of the rustic a diversion from the niceties of classical culture' (p. vii).

roarious fun, crude to be sure, as boarding school humour still is, loudly coarse, childishly naughty. Such 'meaning' as it may convey emanates from its witty parody of classical types coupled with a Humanistic fondness for proverbs, *exempla*, and 'feast of fools' entertainments, and its dramatization of ignorance and folly. But it is as misguided for post-Freudian critics to descant upon 'the aesthetics of scatology' in such a work as this (Swift is a different case) as it was for Bradley, Brett-Smith and their contemporaries to cluck their tongues at the taste of our primitive ancestors. An old English proverbial expression, that something is 'not worth a needle', provides the key to the play's 'meaning'.[21] It is a brilliant trifle, a learned jape, written, perhaps, on a college common room wager: 'I'll bet you that I can write a classical five-act comedy on any subject you care to name.' 'You're on. How about – a needle?' The mysterious Mr. S. would have won his wager handsomely.

STAGING

'Played on stage not long ago in Christ's College in Cambridge.'

This is the first English play of which it is stated that it was played 'on stage'. The earliest specific reference to a stage in a Cambridge college hall occurs in the Christ's accounts for 1529–30: a carpenter received sixteen pence 'for settyng up the stages ij tymes'.[22] In 1551–2, among expenses for Sir Stevenson's play, a carpenter was paid 'for removing the tables in the haull & setting them up ageine with the houses & other thinges'; Nelson speculates that this may have been *Gammer Gurton's Needle*: houses are indeed called for in this play, Gammer Gurton's and Dame Chat's. In *The Staging of Plays before Shakespeare*, Richard Southern illustrates, with copious drawings, how Tudor great halls, whether in palaces, colleges or large manor houses, might be converted into *ad hoc* theatres. Sometimes complete theatres were constructed, as on the occasion of royal visits, with both stage and galleries for the spectators, a special centrally-placed box being set up for the distinguished visitor. More commonly, a low platform, or footpace, was set up at the lower end of the hall, in front of the screens dividing the hall from a transverse passage and the kitchens beyond. The two (rarely three) openings in the screens could serve as entrances for actors onto the stage (or merely into the open playing area on the floor itself if no platform was provided). It is clear from the many college

---

[21] As in *Ancrene Wisse*, ed. Geoffrey Shepherd (1959), p. 25, l. 39.
[22] Alan H. Nelson, *Early Cambridge Theatres: College, University, and Town Stages, 1464–1720* (Cambridge, 1994), p. 65.

accounts that survive, that such structures could involve considerable carpentry and a substantial amount of material (Nelson, *Early Cambridge Theatres, passim*).

Southern accords special attention to *Gammer Gurton's Needle*, speculating at length as to the various ways in which the set might have been built in the hall of Christ's College. A number of references in the text supply hints as to staging, and even if we cannot be sure, as Southern admits, we can gain some notion of how the play may have been presented.[23] Diccon cries 'Make here a little roomth' (II.iv.2), presumably addressing spectators standing near one of the entrances through which the actors came and went, and at III.iii.36, Hodge warns spectators to stand out of the way lest he strike some of them with his staff in the dark. Clearly some members of the audience were very near if not actually on the playing area; thus a large, elevated stage, separate from the spectator area, seems out of the question. There are numerous references to doors and doorposts; this strongly suggests that houses, or at least their façades, with doors, were built on the set. Both Gammer Gurton and Dame Chat have houses, and various characters come from and go into them in the course of the action. Furthermore, action occurs within the houses, apparently out of sight of the audience but reported and commented upon by a character standing outside looking in: Hodge's encounter with Gib the cat inside Gammer's house in I.v, reported by Cock, and Doctor Rat's unfortunate adventure in the darkness in Dame Chat's house in IV.iv, with commentary by Diccon. In both cases, no doubt, appropriate sound effects were supplied.

The set for *Gammer Gurton's Needle* calls for at least one other entrance, besides those for the two houses. There are a number of entrances and exits from and to a place other than the two dwellings: Diccon at I.i, II.i, II.v, IV.iv, V.ii; Hodge at I.ii, II.iii, III.i; Tib at I.iv, I.v; Cock at III.iii and iv; Doctor Rat at IV.i, IV.iv, V.i; Bailey and Scapethrift at V.i, Scapethrift again in V.ii. This 'elsewhere' is vaguely and variously 'the other end of town', the fields where Hodge has been working, or wherever Diccon is imagined to come from at the beginning. If the two houses were set up immediately in front of the two hall screen doors, another entrance would be needed. T. W. Craik says that there was an additional side doorway in the lower end of Christ's College hall before it was extensively remodelled in the eighteenth century.[24] If so, this might

---

[23] Richard Southern, *The Staging of Plays before Shakespeare* (1973), pp. 399–423. The commentary to the present edition notes staging features as they appear in the text.

[24] T. W. Craik, *The Tudor Interlude* (Leicester, 1958), p. 14.

have provided the third way in and out. If not, the 'wings', or the off-stage area on either side of the stage must have been used. Another special design feature is called for, the hole in Dame Chat's house into which Doctor Rat, lured by Diccon, crawls in IV.iv. If a three-dimensional set was constructed, with the houses projecting out into the hall, such an opening could have been provided on the side of Chat's house, and Rat's entry and rapid exit seen in profile by at least part of the audience out front (see Southern's various proposals, pp. 415–21). In the Medieval Players' 1982 production, a simple curtained booth was used, and Rat's feet could be seen projecting from the side of the booth and thrashing about as he was beaten from inside.

One further special feature of the play is to be noted. It has to do both with the mode of dramatic representation and with the actual conditions in which the play was probably originally performed. There are repeated allusions in the text to the lack of light or the need for a candle, and to the difficulty in seeing in the dim light both within the houses and outside. A torch-lit hall at night was still dimly lit by modern standards; pauses between the acts allowed for trimming of tapers and replacing those that had burnt down. This practice was common in the indoor commercial theatres of the Jacobean period such as the Blackfriars as well as in the great private halls that sometimes served as theatres. In a play in which seeking for a minuscule lost object is a major part of the action, it is not surprising for characters to speak of needing more light. They may sometimes simply be making a virtue of necessity, referring outside the play world to the real obscurity of the hall itself, as Hodge certainly does at III.iii.36. There is much to suggest though that semi-darkness is also being represented, that it is evening, and later, night time. Hodge might need a candle to search the loft of the cottage even in daylight, but it is, according to Cock, so dark that Hodge can see nothing and mistakes Gib's eyes for glowing coals. Gammer calls off the search (I.v.57) until 'another time, when we have more light'; this marks the end of the act, when the torches in the hall would be trimmed or renewed. Diccon, although he is fabricating, alleges that he has seen Chat sewing by candlelight with Gammer's needle. Hodge says he has eaten nothing 'this live-long day' (II.i.18); Gammer vows to make Chat 'curse this night' (III.iii.22); Diccon convinces Chat that Hodge will rob her hen-house 'this same night' (IV.iii.34), and Chat later speaks of having been warned of the danger to her poultry 'this afternoon' (V.ii.41). When Doctor Rat is accusing Chat of assault, he states that it was 'within these two hours' (V.ii.29), and the darkness inside her house at the time is alluded to twice (V.i.16; V.ii.25–6). Gammer vows at the end not to 'rest this night' until she has bought drinks for all (V.ii.323).

It is evident then that the author set his play deliberately in the twilight and evening hours, when mistaking and misprising, essential to the comedy of errors, are all too easy. He thus exploited the very conditions prevailing in his theatre at the time of performance. This is the first example of such an emphatically nocturnal setting in English drama. The shadowy Mr. S. was even more innovative than has been supposed.[25] It is scarcely necessary to observe that in a Humanistic text such as this the darkness may also be metaphorical, with ignorant souls groping about blindly, believing any rumour that comes to their ears, lashing out at their neighbours in their frustration, as they seek ever more frantically for some trivial thing that is not lost at all.

THIS EDITION

The text is based on the 1575 quarto (Q), which survives in the exceptionally large number of eleven copies. When preparing the 1984 New Mermaid edition of *Gammer Gurton's Needle*, I consulted almost all of the extant copies. One group of copies have two glaring errors on the title-page: 'anp' and 'Imprented', as in the reproduction from the Chapin Library, Williams College copy in the present volume. This group includes the British Museum and Huntington Library as well as the Chapin copies; the second, larger group showing corrected title-pages and a few corrected misprints in the text, includes copies in the Bodleian, Victoria and Albert (Dyce Collection), Folger and New York Public Library collections. But these corrected copies also 'discorrect' a small number of readings that are correct in the first group (see Brett-Smith, p. xii). Both groups share a large number of misprints, incorrect or missing speech prefixes, and other evidence of careless printing: worn and broken letters, uneven inking, inverted founts, omitted words, etc. There is a great deal of emendation to be done by an editor of this play text. Its markedly imperfect state is yet another problem to add to those of its uncertain authorship, date and early history. The edition of 1661 is apparently a reprint of a copy, possibly Francis Kirkman's, from the 'uncorrected' (BM) group; it preserves that group's 'what' for 'wyth' at I.ii.16, for example. It thus has no authority.

The present modern-spelling edition retains obsolete words; it is not a translation into modern English. But archaic forms of words still current have been modernized to conform to *OED*'s entry

---

[25] See the detailed study of this aspect of the play by Jean-Marie Maguin in *La Nuit dans le Théâtre de Shakespeare et de ses Prédécesseurs*, 2 vols (Lille, 1980), I, 174–89.

forms; this should facilitate any lexicographical research the reader may wish to undertake. Spelling in Q is very inconsistent; it has been normalized in this edition. Where modernization of an archaic form results in loss of rhyme, this is indicated by a note (e.g., *well/nee'le* where Q has *weele/neele*). The dialect has been left largely as it is in Q; the alternatives would have appeared odd and artificial in a modern-spelling text. Rather than sprinkle the text with apostrophes (e.g., '*ch-* for *ch-*), I have retained the elided forms (*cham* = ich am, *chave* = ich have), and glossed each form at its first occurrence and occasionally thereafter if there is possibility of confusion. Sometimes I have regularized a Q dialect form to accord with its own normal practice. In the case of *ichold* and *ichould*, I have had to decide in each instance whether 'ich hold', 'ich could', 'ich would', or 'ich should' is meant, and have tried to make it clear each time by rendering the dialectal form in a distinct modern equivalent. Textual notes indicate all such emendations. 'Needle' occurs as both *neele* and *nedle*; I use the modern spelling when the word is bisyllabic, 'nee'le' when it is monosyllabic. The usual conventions of modern spelling (*i* for *j*, *u* for *v*, etc.) have been observed.

I continue to believe that it is not the job of the editor to direct the play on the pages of the text itself. I prefer to comment on matters of staging and make suggestions in notes. Thus editorial stage directions have been kept to a minimum, although I have adopted in this new edition a few of Tydeman's indications which help to clarify action that is implied by the dialogue. A number of explanatory directions are printed in Q; these of course are retained verbatim. As was customary in the mid-sixteenth century, the quarto prints the names of all characters who appear in a scene at the head of the scene; an editor must add entrances and exists at the appropriate places. Where the appropriate place is a matter of conjecture, this is indicated in a note.

FURTHER READING AND REFERENCE WORKS

Joel B. Altman, *The Tudor Play of Mind* (Berkeley, California, 1978)

T. W. Baldwin, *Shakespere's Five-Act Structure* (Urbana, Illinois, 1947)

J. E. Bernard, Jr., *Prosody of the Tudor Interlude* (New Haven, 1939; repr. New York, 1969)

David Bevington, *From 'Mankind' to Marlowe* (Cambridge, Mass., 1962)

F. S. Boas, *University Drama in the Tudor Age* (Oxford, 1914)

M. C. Bradbrook, *The Growth and Structure of Elizabethan Comedy* (1955)

T. W. Craik, *The Tudor Interlude* (Leicester, 1958)

R. W. Dent, *Proverbial Language in English Drama Exclusive of Shakespeare, 1495–1616: An Index* (Berkeley, 1984)

Douglas Duncan, 'Gammer Gurton's Needle and the Concept of Humanist Parody', *SEL*, 27 (1987), 177–96

William Hazlitt, *Lectures on the Dramatic Literature of the Age of Elizabeth* (1820), Lecture V, in *Complete Works of William Hazlitt*, ed. P. P. Howe, 21 vols (1930–34), VI

Marvin T. Herrick, *Comic Theory in the Sixteenth Century* (Urbana, Illinois, 1950; repr. 1964)

R. W. Ingram, 'Gammer Gurton's Needle: Comedy Not Quite of the Lowest Order?', *SEL*, 7 (1967), 257–68

Jean-Marie Maguin, *La Nuit dans le Théâtre de Shakespeare et de ses Prédécesseurs*, 2 vols (Lille, 1980)

G. C. Moore Smith, *College Plays Performed in the University of Cambridge* (Cambridge, 1921)

Alan H. Nelson, 'Contexts for Early English Drama: The Universities', in *Contexts for Early English Drama*, ed. Marianne G. Briscoe and John C. Coldewey (Bloomington, Indiana, 1989), pp. 137–49

Alan H. Nelson, *Early Cambridge Theatres: College, University and Town Stages, 1464–1720* (Cambridge, 1994)

Alan H. Nelson, ed., *Cambridge*, Records of Early English Drama, 2 vols (Toronto, 1989)

Howard B. Norland, *Drama in Early Tudor Britain 1485–1558* (Lincoln, Nebraska, 1995)

J. W. Robinson, 'The Art and Meaning of Gammer Gurton's Needle', *RenD*, n.s. 14 (1983), 45–77

A. P. Rossiter, *English Drama from Early Times to the Elizabethans* (1950)

Norman Sanders, Richard Southern, T. W. Craik, and Lois Potter, *The Revels History of Drama in English*, volume II: 1500–1576 (1980)

Richard Southern, *The Staging of Plays before Shakespeare* (1973)

Bernard Spivack, *Shakespeare and the Allegory of Evil* (1958)

William B. Toole, 'The Aesthetics of Scatology in *Gammer Gurton's Needle*', *ELN*, 10 (1973), 252–8

Charles Whitworth, 'Reporting Offstage Events in Early Tudor Drama', forthcoming in *Conventions of Tudor Drama*, volume IV of *Collection Theta: Essays on Semiotics of the Theatre* (Université François Rabelais-Tours), gen. ed. André Lascombes (Bern, 1997)

Glynne Wickham, *Early English Stages 1300–1660*, 3 vols (1959–81). Esp. vol. III, ch. viii: 'English Comedy from its Origins to 1576'.

F. P. Wilson, *The English Drama 1485–1585*, Oxford History of English Literature, IV, part i (1969)

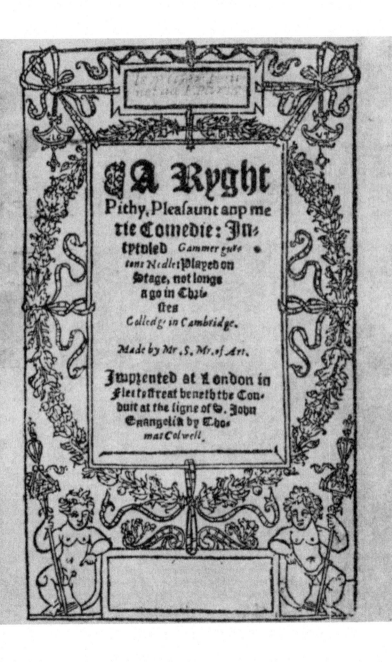

¶A Ryght
Pithy, Pleasaunt and me
rie Comedie: In=
tytuled Gammer gure
tons Nedle: Played on
Stage, not longe
a go in Chri=
stes
Colledge in Cambridge.

Made by Mr. S. Mr. of Art.

Imprinted at London in
Fletstreat beneth the Con=
duit at the signe of S. John
Euangelist by Tho=
mas Colwell.

The names of the Speakers in this Comedy

DICCON, *the Bedlam*
HODGE, *Gammer Gurton's servant*
TIB, *Gammer Gurton's maid*
GAMMER GURTON
COCK, *Gammer Gurton's boy*
DAME CHAT
DOCTOR RAT, *the curate*
MASTER BAILEY
DOLL, *Dame Chat's maid*
SCAPETHRIFT, *Mast' Bailey's servant*
[GIB, *Gammer Gurton's cat*]
Mutes

God Save the Queen

2 *the Bedlam* (i.e. Bethlehem) Originally the Hospital of St Mary of Bethlehem in London, founded in the 13th century as a priory, and by the time of the play, a royal foundation for the care of the mentally ill. Inmates of the hospital, and by extension, any insane person, came to be called by its name. Partially-cured patients were often discharged, with a licence to beg and a tin plate as an identifying badge. Hence, the term came to be loosely employed to refer to beggars and vagrants as well as madmen.

6 COCK eds. (Docke Q)
boy houseboy

7 CHAT Both the English verb and the French for 'cat' (*chat*; feminine form, *chatte*).

8 *curate* Either the incumbent priest or parson of a parish, or a deputy, a clergyman licensed by the bishop to perform the incumbent's duties in his place. The latter usage is peculiar to the Church of England, and first occurs in the mid-16th century (*OED*); the incumbent is now usually called 'vicar'. Doctor Rat is obviously the parish priest (IV.i.2) and is, in fact, called both 'parson' (III.iii.59) and 'vicar' (IV.ii.1; V.ii.262).

9 BAILEY The bailiff (whence the proper name), a local sheriff's officer who executes writs, makes arrests, etc.

11 *Mast'* ed. (mayst Q) Master

13 *Mutes* Presumably neighbours and townspeople who gather to watch scenes like the fight in III.iii and the finale (V.ii), though no reference is made in the text to persons other than the principals. In fact, Doll and Scapethrift, though named, are mutes; they are given no lines to speak.

14 *the Queen* Elizabeth I. This refers to the time of publication (1575) rather than to that of composition and performance. See Introduction, pp. xi–xii.

The Prologue

As Gammer Gurton, with many a wide stitch
Sat piecing and patching of Hodge her man's breech,
By chance or misfortune as she her gear tossed,
In Hodge's leather breeches her needle she lost.
When Diccon the Bedlam had heard by report   5
That good Gammer Gurton was robbed in this sort,
He quietly persuaded with her in that stound
Dame Chat, her dear gossip, this needle had found;
Yet knew she no more of this matter, alas,
Than knoweth Tom our clerk what the priest saith at mass.   10
Hereof there ensued so fearful a fray,
Mas' Doctor was sent for, these gossips to stay,
Because he was curate and esteemed full wise;
Who found that he sought not, by Diccon's device.
When all things were tumbled and clean out of fashion,   15
Whether it were by fortune or some other constellation,
Suddenly the nee'le Hodge found by the pricking
And drew it out of his buttock where he felt it sticking,
Their hearts then at rest with perfect security,
With a pot of good nale they struck up their *plaudite*.   20

---

2 *piecing* mending
  breech (now used only in plural, *breeches*) trousers; also, specifically, the trousers
  seat
3 *her gear tossed* went about her work
7 *persuaded with* convinced
  in that stound at that time
8 *gossip* familiar acquaintance
9 *she* (i.e., Dame Chat)
10 *Than ... mass* The clerk would have been a member of a 'minor order', i.e., in-
   ferior to deacons and priests, who assisted the priest in the various services. He
   would have had little or no formal theological training, hence might not have
   understood the Latin used by the priest. The reputed ignorance of the lower
   clergy, including parish priests, was notorious and from the later Middle Ages
   was a common theme in literature.
12 *Mas'* Master
   stay restrain or pacify
15 *tumbled ... fashion* utterly chaotic
16 *constellation* In astrology, the positions of planets in relation to one another is
   supposed to exert influence on earthly events.
17 *nee'le* (neele Q)
20 *nale* ale
   plaudite (L., *applaud*) appeal for applause at the end of a play or other performance

Act I, Scene i

[*Enter* DICCON]

DICCON

Many a mile have I walked, divers and sundry ways,
And many a good man's house have I been at in my days,
Many a gossip's cup in my time have I tasted,
And many a broach and spit have I both turned and
      basted.
Many a piece of bacon have I had out of their balks,   5
In running over the country with long and weary walks.
Yet came my foot never within those door cheeks
To seek flesh or fish, garlic, onions or leeks,
That ever I saw a sort in such a plight
As here within this house appeareth to my sight.   10
There is howling and scowling, all cast in a dump,
With whewling and puling as though they had lost a
      trump;
Sighing and sobbing, they weep and they wail –
I marvel in my mind what the devil they ail!
The old trot sits groaning with 'Alas!' and 'Alas!'   15
And Tib wrings her hands and takes on in worse case.
With poor Cock, their boy, they be driven in such fits,
I fear me the folks be not well in their wits.
Ask them what they ail, or who brought them in this stay,
They answer not at all but 'Alack and wellaway!'   20
When I saw it booted not, out at doors I hied me

---

0 s.d. Diccon enters from somewhere other than the two houses, obviously, as
  does Hodge in the next scene. See the discussion of staging in the Introduction.
4 *broach* pointed instrument for roasting meat upon, a spit
5 *balks* Tie-beams of houses, stretching from wall to wall. In one-storey houses,
  boards would be laid across these, forming a loft, or balk, in which dried food
  and other articles were stored.
7 *cheeks* side-posts or uprights of a door
9 *sort* group of people
11 *cast . . . dump* melancholy, depressed
12 *whewling and puling* moaning and whining
   lost a trump (i.e., in a card game)
15 *trot* hag
20 *Alack and wellaway* (exclamation of sorrow)
21 *booted not* was to no avail   *hied me* took myself

And caught a slip of bacon when I saw that none spied
    me,
Which I intend not far hence, unless my purpose fail,
Shall serve for a shoeing-horn to draw on two pots of ale.

Act I, Scene ii

[Enter HODGE]

HODGE
See, so cham arrayed with dabbling in the dirt –
She that set me to ditching, ich would she had the squirt!
Was never poor soul that such a life had.
Gog's bones, this vilthy glay has dressed me too bad!
God's soul, see how this stuff tears –   5
Ich were better to be bearward and set to keep bears!
By the mass, here is a gash, a shameful hole indeed;
And one stitch tear further, a man may thrust in his head!
DICCON
By my father's soul, Hodge, if I should now be sworn,
I cannot choose but say thy breech is foul betorn.   10
But the next remedy in such a case and hap
Is to planch on a piece as broad as thy cap.
HODGE
Gog's soul, man, 'tis not yet two days fully ended
Since my dame Gurton, cham sure, these breeches
    amended;
But cham made such a drudge to trudge at every need,   15
Chwould rend it though it were stitched with sturdy
    packthread.

22 *slip* slice

1 *cham* (dialect) I am
1–2 Hodge is apparently a field labourer. Gammer Gurton is reasonably well-to-
   do: she maintains three servants, and has a cow and a sow at least (IV.i.22).
2 *ich* (dialect) I   *squirt* diarrhoea
4 *Gog's bones* by God's bones. 'Gog's' is a common corrupt form of 'God's'.
   vilthy glay (dialect) filthy clay
8 *and* if
11 *next* nearest
12 *planch . . . piece* clap on a patch
16 *Chwould* ed. (chwold Q) I would
   packthread ed. (pacthreede Q)

DICCON

    Hodge, let thy breeches go, and speak and tell me soon,
    What devil aileth Gammer Gurton and Tib her maid to
        frown.

HODGE

    Tush, man th'art deceived, 'tis their daily look;
    They cower so over the coals, their eyes be bleared with
        smoke.   20

DICCON

    Nay, by the mass, I perfectly perceived as I came hither
    That either Tib and her dame hath been by the ears
        together,
    Or else as great a matter, as thou shalt shortly see.

HODGE

    Now ich beseech our Lord they never better agree!

DICCON

    By Gog's soul, there they sit as still as stones in the
        street,   25
    As though they had been taken with fairies or else with
        some ill sprite.

HODGE

    Gog's heart, I durst have laid my cap to a crown
    Chwould learn of some prancome as soon as ich came to
        town.

DICCON

    Why, Hodge, art thou inspired? Or didst thou thereof
        hear?

HODGE

    Nay, but ich saw such a wonder as ich saw not this seven
        year: 30
    Tom Tankard's cow, by Gog's bones, she set me up her
        sail,
    And flinging about his half-acre fisking with her tail
    As though there had been in her arse a swarm of bees –

---

22 *hath* have (the singular form for a plural verb is common)
    by the ears fighting
26 *taken with* possessed, bewitched by
    sprite spirit
27 *durst . . . crown* would dare to wager my cap against a crown (five shillings).
28 *prancome* prank, strange thing
29 *art . . . inspired* do you have supernatural knowledge
31 *set . . . sail* hoisted up her tail (like a sail)
32 *fisking* whisking

And chad not cried, 'Tphrowh, whore!', she 'ad leapt out
   of his leas!

DICCON

Why, Hodge, lies the cunning in Tom Tankard's cow's
   tail?   35

HODGE

Well, chave heard some say such tokens do not fail.
But canst thou not tell, in faith, Diccon, why she frowns
   or whereat?
Hath no man stolen her ducks or hens, or gelded Gib her
   cat?

DICCON

What devil can I tell, man? I could not have one word!
They gave no more heed to my talk than thou wouldst to
   a turd.   40

HODGE

Ich can not still but muse what marvellous thing it is;
Chill in and know myself what matters are amiss.

DICCON

Then farewell, Hodge, awhile, since thou dost inward
   haste,
For I will into the good wife Chat's, to feel how the ale
   doth taste.   [*Exit*]

34 *And chad* If I had   *she 'ad* ed. (shead Q)
   leas pastures

35 *cunning* intelligence

36 *chave* ed. (ich chave Q) I have

40 *turd* ed. (lorde Q) J. C. Maxwell's suggestion (*N&Q*, 190 [1953], 266). The
   same rhyme, with *word*, occurs also at I.v.52–3, where Hodge does give heed to
   a turd. It would be in keeping with a prominent motif in the play, and no editor
   has satisfactorily explained why Diccon should impute to the credulous Hodge,
   of all people, a particular contempt for the nobility. Such usage of the word, con-
   noting worthlessness or triviality, is amply documented in *OED*.

42 *Chill* I'll

44 *Chat's . . . taste* Dame Chat's house is obviously an alehouse, where ale was both
   brewed and sold, and could be consumed on the premises. Originally, brewers
   sold their ale to customers who took it away. Consumption on the premises
   seems to have begun in the late Middle Ages.

44 s.d. *Exit* eds. Where does Diccon go? Chat's door is only a few feet away;
   Diccon's 'into' suggests its proximity. But he clearly does not go there until
   II.ii.19. In the meantime, he is on hand to comment on the song which opens
   Act II and to perform the 'conjuring' scene (II.i) with Hodge. A director might
   resolve the problem by having Diccon stand aside only, and not exit here, so that
   he is 'on' during the song, but his presence onstage during scenes in which he
   does not take part (I.iii, I.iv, I.v) would establish a precedent which would then
   need to be maintained throughout. I follow other editors in providing an exit for
   Diccon; a director will decide how best to do it. See II.i headnote.

Act I, Scene iii

HODGE

    Cham aghast, by the mass, ich wot not what to do –
    Chad need bless me well before ich go them to!
    Perchance some felon sprite may haunt our house indeed,
    And then chwere but a noddy to venture where cha' no
        need.

[Enter TIB]

TIB

    Cham worse than mad, by the mass, to be at this stay!   5
    Cham chid, cham blamed and beaten all th' hours on the
        day;
    Lamed and hunger-starved, pricked up all in jags,
    Having no patch to hide my back, save a few rotten rags.

HODGE

    I say, Tib, if thou be Tib, as I trow sure thou be,
    What devil make-ado is this between our dame and thee?   10

TIB

    Gog's bread, Hodge, thou had a good turn thou wert not
        here this while!
    It had been better for some of us to have been hence a
        mile.
    My Gammer is so out of course and frantic all at once,
    That Cock, our boy, and I, poor wench, have felt it on
        our bones.

HODGE

    What is the matter, say on, Tib, whereat she taketh so
        on?   15

TIB

    She is undone, she saith, alas, her joy and life is gone.
    If she hear not of some comfort, she is, faith, but dead;

  1 *wot* know
  2 *Chad* I had
  4 *chwere* I were
    noddy simpleton
  5 *at this stay* in this predicament
  6 *chid* chided, scolded
  7 *pricked up* dressed
    jags tatters
  9 *trow* believe
 10 *make-ado* uproar (?)
 11 *Gog's bread* (oath) communion bread
 13 *out of course* distracted

Shall never come within her lips one inch of meat ne
    bread.

HODGE

By'r Lady, cham not very glad to see her in this dump –
Chold a noble her stool hath fallen and she hath broke
    her rump!   20

TIB

Nay, and that were the worst, we would not greatly care,
For bursting of her huckle-bone or breaking of her chair;
But greater, greater is her grief, as, Hodge, we shall all
    feel.

HODGE

Gog's wounds, Tib, my Gammer has never lost her
    nee'le?

TIB

Her nee'le!

HODGE   Her nee'le?   25

TIB

Her nee'le, by him that made me! It is true, Hodge, I tell
    thee!

HODGE

Gog's sacrament, I would she had lost th'heart out of her
    belly!
The devil or else his dam, they ought her sure a shame!
How a murrain came this chance, say, Tib, unto our
    dame?

TIB

My Gammer sat her down on her pess and bad me reach
    thy breeches,   30
And by and by – a vengeance on it! – or she had take two
    stitches
To clap a clout upon thine arse, by chance aside she leers,

18 *ne* nor
20 *Chold* I hold, wager
    noble gold coin worth six shillings and eight pence
22 *bursting* breaking
    huckle-bone hip-bone
28 *dam* ed. (dame Q) mother
    ought owed
29 *murrain* ed. (murryon Q) plague
    how a murrain how the devil
30 *pess* hassock or cushion
31 *or* before
32 *clout* patch
    leers glances

And Gib, our cat, in the milk pan she spied, over head
    and ears.
'Ah, whore! Out, thief!' she cried aloud, and swapped the
    breeches down;
Up went her staff and out leapt Gib at doors into the
    town,   35
And since that time was never wight could set their eyes
    upon it.
Gog's malison chave, Cock and I, bid twenty times light
    on it!

HODGE

And is not then my breeches sewed up, tomorrow that I
    should wear?

TIB

No, in faith, Hodge, thy breeches lie for all this never the
    near.

HODGE

Now a vengeance light on all the sort that better should
    have kept it –   40
The cat, the house, and Tib our maid that better should
    have swept it!

[Enter GAMMER GURTON]

See where she cometh crawling – come on, in twenty
    devils' way!
Ye have made a fair day's work, have you not! Pray you,
    say!

Act I, Scene iv

GAMMER GURTON

Alas, Hodge, alas! I may well curse and ban
This day that ever I saw it, with Gib and the milk pan;
For these and ill luck together, as knoweth Cock, my boy,

---

34 *swapped* slapped
36 *wight* person
37 *Gog's . . . it* Cock and I have prayed twenty times that God's curse light upon the
    needle.
39 *never the near* no nearer completion
41 s.d. Q, as usual, simply lists Gammer Gurton's name with the others at the be-
    ginning of scene iv. But she is undoubtedly visible to the audience at l. 42.
42 *in twenty devils' way* an expression of impatience

1 *ban* curse

Have stack away my dear nee'le and robbed me of my
    joy,
My fair long straight nee'le that was mine only treasure.   5
The first day of my sorrow is, and last end of my pleasure.

HODGE

Might ha' kept it when ye had it, but fools will be fools
    still!
Lose that is vast in your hands ye need not, but ye will!

GAMMER GURTON

Go hie thee, Tib, and run, thou whore, to th'end here of
    the town;
Didst carry out dust in thy lap – seek where thou
    pouredst it down,   10
And as thou sawest me raking in the ashes where I
    mourned,
So see in all the heap of dust thou leave no straw
    unturned.

TIB

That chall, Gammer, swith and tite, and soon be here
    again!

GAMMER GURTON

Tib, stoop and look down to the ground – to it, and take
    some pain!

                         [*Exit* TIB]

HODGE

Here is a pretty matter, to see this gear how it goes;   15
By Gog's soul, I think you would lose your arse and it
    were loose!
Your nee'le lost? It is pity you should lack care and
    endless sorrow!
Gog's death, how shall my breeches be sewed? Shall I go
    thus tomorrow?

---

  4 *stack* struck
  7 *fools . . . still* Proverbial (Tilley F547)
  8 *vast* (dialect) fast
10 *pouredst* ed. (porest Q)
11 *raking* ed. (roking Q; rucking (i.e. crouching) eds)
13 *chall* I shall
    swith and tite quickly, right away
14 *ground – to it* ed. (ground to it Q)
15 *gear* business

GAMMER GURTON

    Ah, Hodge, Hodge, if that ich could find my nee'le, by
        the reed,

    Chwould sew thy breeches, ich promise thee, with full
        good double thread,   20

    And set a patch on either knee, should last these months
        twain

    Now God and good Saint Sithe I pray to send it home
        again!

HODGE

    Whereto served your hands and eyes but this your nee'le
        to keep?

    What devil had you else to do? Ye kept, ich wot, no
        sheep!

    Cham fain abroad to dig and delve in water, mire and
        clay,   25

    Sossing and possing in the dirt still from day to day.

    A hundred things that be abroad, cham set to see them
        well,

    And four of you sit idle at home and cannot keep a nee'le!

GAMMER GURTON

    My nee'le, alas, ich lost it, Hodge, what time ich me up
        hasted

    To save the milk set up for thee, which Gib our cat hath
        wasted.   30

HODGE

    The devil he burst both Gib and Tib, with all the rest!

    Cham always sure of the worst end, whoever have the
        best!

    Where ha' you been fidging abroad since you your nee'le
        lost?

GAMMER GURTON

    Within the house and at the door, sitting by this same
        post,

---

19 *reed* rood, cross
20 *Chwould* ed. (Chould Q) I would
21 *months* eds. (monethes Q)
22 *Saint Sithe* Saint Osyth, a seventh-century East Saxon queen who founded a
    nunnery at Chich (now called Saint Osyth) in Essex, said to have been martyred
    by the Danes.
25 *fain* obliged
26 *sossing and possing* splashing and tramping
27 *well* ed. (weele Q)
28 *four of you* (i.e. Gammer, Tib, Cock, Gib the cat)
31 *The devil he* May the devil
33 *fidging* moving about restlessly

Where I was looking a long hour before these folks came
    here.   35
But wellaway, all was in vain, my nee'le is never the near!
HODGE
Set me a candle, let me seek and grope wherever it be.
Gog's heart, ye be so foolish, ich think, you know it not
    when you it see!
GAMMER GURTON
Come hither, Cock! What, Cock, I say!

                    [*Enter* COCK]

COCK   How, Gammer?
GAMMER GURTON   Go hie thee soon
And grope behind the old brass pan, which thing when
    thou hast done,   40
There shalt thou find an old shoe, wherein if thou look
    well,
Thou shalt find lying an inch of a white tallow candle.
Light it and bring it tite away.
COCK   That shall be done anon.

                    [*Exit into the house*]

GAMMER GURTON
Nay, tarry, Hodge, till thou hast light, and then we'll seek
    each one.
HODGE
Come away, ye whoreson boy! Are ye asleep? Ye must
    have a crier!   45
COCK [*Within*]
Ich cannot get the candle light – here is almost no fire.
HODGE
Chill hold thee a penny chill make ye come if that ich
    may catch thine ears!
Art deaf, thou whoreson boy? Cock, I say! Why, canst not
    hear's?

---

35 *these folks* Referring to the audience. Such frank acknowledgement of the audi-
    ence's presence and proximity (as also at II.iv.2 and III.iii.36) is common in the
    interludes of the period.
36 *near* nearer
42 *candle* eds (candell Q)
43 *anon* immediately

GAMMER GURTON

Beat him not, Hodge, but help the boy and come you two
together.

[*Exit* HODGE *into the house*]

Act I, Scene v

[*Enter* TIB]

GAMMER GURTON

How now, Tib! Quick, let's hear what news thou hast
brought hither.

TIB

Chave tossed and tumbled yonder heap o'er and over
again,

And winnowed it through my fingers as men would
winnow grain.

Not so much as a hen's turd but in pieces I tare it,

Or whatsoever clod or clay I found, I did not spare it.   5

Looking within and eke without to find your nee'le, alas,

But all in vain and without help: your nee'le is where it
was.

GAMMER GURTON

Alas, my nee'le, we shall never meet – adieu, adieu for
aye!

TIB

Not so, Gammer! We might it find if we know where it
lay.

[*Enter* COCK]

COCK

Gog's cross, Gammer, if ye will laugh, look in but at the
door,   10

And see how Hodge lieth tumbling and tossing amidst the
floor,

---

3 *winnowed* sifted

   winnow grain To expose it to a current of air, or sift it, so that the chaff blows
away, leaving the kernel.

4 *tare* tore

6 *eke* also

7 *without help* to no avail

8 *for aye* forever

11 *admist* in the middle of

Raking there some fire to find among the ashes dead
Where there is not one spark so big as a pin's head.
At last, in a dark corner, two sparks he thought he sees,
Which were indeed nought else but Gib our cat's two
    eyes.   15
'Puff!' quoth Hodge, thinking thereby to have fire
    without doubt;
With that Gib shut her two eyes and so the fire was out,
And by and by them opened even as they were before.
With that the sparks appeared even as they had done of
    yore;
And even as Hodge blew the fire, as he did think,   20
Gib, as she felt the blast, straightway began to wink,
Till Hodge fell of swearing, as came best to his turn,
The fire was sure bewitched and therefore would not
    burn.
At last Gib up the stairs, among the old posts and pins,
And Hodge, he hied him after till broke were both his
    shins,   25
Cursing and swearing oaths were never of his making,
That Gib would fire the house if that she were not taken!
GAMMER GURTON
    See, here is all the thought that the foolish urchin taketh,
    And Tib, methink, at his elbow almost as merry
        maketh. –
    This is all the wit ye have when others make their moan!   30
    Come down, Hodge! Where art thou? And let the cat
        alone.
HODGE [*Within*]
    Gog's heart, help and come up! Gib in her tail hath fire,
    And is like to burn all if she get a little higher.
    'Come down', quoth you? Nay, then you might count me
        a patch –
    The house cometh down on your heads if it take once the
        thatch.   35
GAMMER GURTON
    It is the cat's eyes, fool, that shineth in the dark.
HODGE [*Within*]
    Hath the cat, do you think, in every eye a spark?

19 *of yore* before
22 *fell of* began
  as . . . turn such oaths as best served his purpose
26 *were . . . making* that he certainly did not invent
34 *patch* fool, dolt

GAMMER GURTON

No, but they shine as like fire as ever man see.

HODGE [*Within*]

By the mass, and she burn all, you sh' bear the blame for
    me!

GAMMER GURTON

Come down and help to seek here our nee'le that it were
    found.   40

Down, Tib, on thy knees, I say! Down, Cock, to the
    ground!

[They kneel]

To God I make a vow, and so to good Saint Anne:
A candle shall they have apiece, get it where I can,
If I may my nee'le find in one place or in other.

[Enter HODGE from the house]

HODGE

Now a vengeance on Gib light, on Gib and Gib's mother,   45
And all the generation of cats both far and near! –
Look on the ground, whoreson! Thinks thou the nee'le is
    here?

COCK

By my troth, Gammer, methought your nee'le here I saw,
But when my fingers touched it, I felt it was a straw.

TIB

See, Hodge, what's this? May it not be within it?   50

HODGE

Break it, fool, with thy hand, and see and thou canst find
    it.

TIB

Nay, break it you, Hodge, according to your word.

HODGE

Gog's sides! Fie, it stinks! It is a cat's turd!

39 *you sh'* ed. (yoush Q) you shall

    you . . . me it will be your fault, as far as I'm concerned

41 *thy* eds (tho Q)

41 s.d. Tydeman

42 *Saint Anne* (or Hannah) Traditionally, the name of the Virgin Mary's mother.
    She is a character in several plays of the *N-town* mystery cycle (15th century).

46 *generation* race

47 This line is addressed to Cock. It and the following dialogue imply that Tib and
    Cock have picked objects from Hodge's clothing; he has been 'tumbling and
    tossing amidst the floor'.

It were well done to make thee eat it, by the mass!
GAMMER GURTON
    This matter amendeth not, my nee'le is still where it was.   55
    Our candle is at an end. Let us all in quite,
    And come another time, when we have more light.

                    [*Exeunt*]

Act II

First a Song

    Back and side, go bare, go bare,
        Both foot and hand go cold;
    But Belly, God send thee good ale enough,
        Whether it be new or old.

    I can not eat but little meat,   5
        My stomach is not good;
    But sure I think that I can drink
        With him that wears a hood.
    Though I go bare take ye no care,
        I am nothing a-cold: 10
    I stuff my skin so full within
        Of jolly good ale and old.

    Back and side, go bare, go bare,
        Both foot and hand go cold;
    But Belly, God send thee good ale enough,   15
        Whether it be new or old.

56–7 A clear signal that a pause is to follow. The song fills the pause, and the action resumes with Diccon's entrance.

First a Song There is nothing to indicate who sings the song, but it clearly was sung, as Diccon thanks the performers in II.i.i. A full version is given by Alexander Dyce in his edition of John Skelton's *Works* (1843), I, vii–ix, from a manuscript. It is reprinted as an appendix in Brett-Smith's edition of the play (pp. 71–4). Ralph Vaughan Williams set the song in Act I of his opera, *Sir John in Love* (1929), based on *The Merry Wives of Windsor*.
  8 *him that wears a hood* Probably a monk or friar, with satirical implication.

I love no roast but a nut-brown toast
    And a crab laid in the fire;
A little bread shall do me stead,
    Much bread I not desire.   20
No frost nor snow no wind I trow,
    Can hurt me if I would;
I am so wrapped and throughly lapped
    Of jolly good ale and old.

Back and side go bare, etc.   25

And Tib my wife, that as her life
    Loveth well good ale to seek,
Full oft drinks she till ye may see
    The tears run down her cheeks.
Then doth she troll to me the bowl,   30
    Even as a malt-worm should;
And saith, 'Sweetheart, I took my part
    Of this jolly good ale and old'.

Back and side go bare, etc.

Now let them drink till they nod and wink   35
    Even as good fellows should do;
They shall not miss to have the bliss
    Good ale doth bring men to.
And all poor souls that have scoured bowls,
    Or have them lustily trolled,   40
God save the lives of them and their wives,
    Whether they be young or old.

Back and side go bare, etc.

18 *crab* crab-apple
    crab . . . fire Probably for lamb's-wool, a hot drink made with the pulp of roasted apples or crab-apples and ale. See Peele, *The Old Wife's Tale*, ed. C. Whitworth, New Mermaid (1996), ll. 61–2, note.
19 *do me stead* suffice me
23 *throughly lapped* thoroughly enfolded
30 *troll . . . bowl* pass it to me
31 *malt-worm* (figuratively) lover of malt-liquor
39 *scoured* emptied by drinking

Act II, Scene i

[*Enter* DICCON]

DICCON

Well done, by Gog's malt, well sung and well said!
Come on, Mother Chat, as thou art true maid,
One fresh pot of ale let's see, to make an end,
Against this cold weather my naked arms to defend.
This gear it warms the soul – now wind, blow on the
    worst,   5
And let us drink and swill till that our bellies burst!
Now were he a wise man by cunning could define
Which way my journey lieth or where Diccon will dine.
But one good turn I have, be it by night or day,
South, East, North or West, I am never out of my way.   10

[*Enter* HODGE]

HODGE

Cham goodly rewarded, am I not, do you think?
Chad a goodly dinner for all my sweat and swink:
Neither butter, cheese, milk, onions, flesh nor fish,
Save this poor piece of barley bread – 'tis a pleasant costly
    dish!

DICCON

Hail, fellow Hodge, and well to fare with thy meat, if
    thou have any;   15
But by thy words as I them smelled, thy daintrels be not
    many.

---

0 s.d. *Enter* DICCON. Some editors have Diccon enter with a pot of ale from Dame
   Chat's (Adams, Creeth, Tydeman). This would account for his absence since
   I.ii, especially since he has said that is where he was going (I.ii.44) and seems
   appropriate in support of lines 1–6 here. But his greeting to Dame Chat and her
   reply in II.ii.19–24 strongly suggest that their first meeting in the play occurs
   then. See I.ii.44 n.

1 *by Gog's malt* Earliest recorded occurrence of this nonce-oath, obviously
   suggested by the preceding song.

6 *swill* guzzle

11 *Cham* ed. (chym Q)   *am* ed. (cham Q; here and occasionally elsewhere in Q
   the dialectic *ch-* form is used superfluously)

12 *swink* toil

16 *smelled* understood
   daintrels dainties

HODGE

> Daintrels, Diccon? Gog's soul, man, save this piece of dry
>   horse-bread,
> Cha' bit no bite this livelong day, no crumb come in my
>   head.
> My guts they yawl, crawl and all my belly rumbleth,
> The puddings cannot lie still, each one over other
>   tumbleth.   20
> By Gog's heart, cham so vexed, and in my belly penned,
> Chwould one piece were at the spitalhouse, another at the
>   castle's end!

DICCON

> Why Hodge, was there none at home thy dinner for to
>   set?

HODGE

> Gog's bread, Diccon, ich came too late; was nothing
>   there to get!
> Gib – a foul fiend might on her light! – licked the milk
>   pan so clean,   25
> See, Diccon, 'twas not so well washed this seven year, as
>   ich ween.
> A pestilence light on all ill luck! Chad thought yet, for all
>   this,
> Of a morsel of bacon behind the door at worst should not
>   miss;
> But when ich sought a slip to cut, as ich was wont to do,
> Gog's soul, Diccon, Gib our cat had eat the bacon too!   30

> *Which bacon Diccon stole, as is declared before*

DICCON

> 'Ill luck', quoth he! Marry, swear it, Hodge, this day, the
>   truth to tell,
> Thou rose not on thy right side, or else blessed thee not
>   well.

---

17 *horse-bread* Coarse bread made of beans, bran, etc., as food for horses. Hodge's
     barley bread (l. 14) would not really be of quite such poor quality.

18 *bite* ed. (byt Q)

19 *yawl, crawl* cry out and writhe in pain

20 *puddings* intestines

22 *spitalhouse* hospital

26 *ween* believe

30 *eat* eaten (pronounced 'et')

30 s.d. *Which ... before* (in Q; refers to I.i.22)

31 *'Ill luck'* Diccon echoes Hodge (line 27).

31–2 *this day ... side* Proverbial (Tilley S246). This just isn't your day.

    Thy milk slopped up, thy bacon filched! That was too bad
       luck, Hodge!

HODGE

    Nay, nay, there was a fouler fault: my Gammer ga' me the
       dodge.

    See'st not how cham rent and torn, my heels, my knees,
       and my breech?   35

    Chad thought as ich sat by the fire, help here and there a
       stitch,

    But there ich was pooped indeed.

DICCON   Why, Hodge?

HODGE   Boots

    not, man, to tell.

    Cham so dressed amongst a sort of fools, chad better be
       in hell!

    My Gammer, cham ashamed to say, by God, served me
       not well.

DICCON

    How so, Hodge?

HODGE   Has she not gone, trowest now, and lost
       her nee'le?   40

DICCON

    Her eel, Hodge? Who fished of late? That was a dainty
       dish!

HODGE

    Tush, tush, her nee'le, her nee'le, her nee'le, man – 'tis
       neither flesh nor fish!

    A little thing with an hole in the end, as bright as any
       silver,

    Small, long, sharp at the point, and straight as any pillar.

DICCON

    I know not what a devil thou meanst! Thou bringst me
       more in doubt.   45

HODGE

    Knowest not with what Tom Tailor's man sits broaching
       through a clout?

    A nee'le, a nee'le, a nee'le! My Gammer's nee'le is gone!

---

34 *ga' me the dodge* tricked me, let me down
37 *pooped* deceived, cheated
    Boots not It's no use
38 *Cham . . . sort* I am so badly served in such company
43 *silver* ed. (siller Q)
46 *broaching* making holes (i.e. sewing)

DICCON

    Her nee'le, Hodge, now I smell thee! That was a chance
        alone!

    By the mass, thou hadst a shameful loss, and it were but
        for thy breeches.

HODGE

    Gog's soul, man, chwould give a crown chad it but three
        stitches!   50

DICCON

    How sayest thou, Hodge! What should he have, again thy
        needle got?

HODGE

    By m' vather's soul, and chad it, chwould give him a new
        groat.

DICCON

    Canst thou keep counsel in this case?

HODGE   Else chwould my

    tongue were out!

DICCON

    Do thou but then by my advice and I will fetch it without
        doubt.

HODGE

    Chill run, chill ride, chill dig, chill delve, chill toil, chill
        trudge, shalt see.   55

    Chill hold, chill draw, chill pull, chill pinch, chill kneel on
        my bare knee.

    Chill scrape, chill scratch, chill sift, chill seek, chill bow,
        chill bend, chill sweat.

    Chill stoop, chill stir, chill cap, chill kneel, chill creep on
        hands and feet.

    Chill be thy bondman, Diccon, ich swear by sun and
        moon,

    And 'ch cannot somewhat to stop this gap, cham utterly
        undone!   60

                    Pointing behind to his torn breeches

DICCON

    Why, is there any special cause thou takest hereat such
        sorrow!

---

52 *vather's* (dialect) father's
    groat a coin worth four pence
58 *cap* take off my cap
60 *'ch cannot* ed. (channot Q)

HODGE
    Kirstian Clack, Tom Simson's maid, by the mass, comes
        hither tomorrow.
    Cham not able to say between us what may hap;
    She smiled on me the last Sunday, when ich put off my
        cap.
DICCON
    Well, Hodge, this is a matter of weight, and must be kept
        close;   65
    It might else turn to both our costs, as the world now
        goes.
    Shalt swear to be no blab, Hodge?
HODGE   Chill, Diccon.
DICCON   Then go to.
    Lay thine hand here [*points to his buttocks*]; say after me as
        thou shalt hear me do.
    Hast no book?
HODGE   Cha' no book, I!
DICCON   Then needs must force us
        both
    Upon my breech to lay thine hand, and there to take
        thine oath.   70
HODGE
    I, Hodge, breechless,
    Swear to Diccon, rechless,
    By the cross that I shall kiss,
    To keep his counsel close
    And always me to dispose   75
    To work that his pleasure is.

Here he kisseth Diccon's breech

DICCON
    Now, Hodge, see thou take heed,
    And do as I thee bid,
    For so I judge it meet;
    This needle again to win,   80
    There is no shift therein

65 *close* secret
67 *go to* let's get on with it
71 From here to II.ii.18, the verse shifts to short lined, tail-rhyme stanzas (*aabccb*).
71–6 Coarse parody of a solemn oath taken on a cross.
72 *rechless* recklessly, without reservation
79 *meet* proper
81 *shift* expedient

But conjure up a sprite.
HODGE
What, the great devil, Diccon, I say?
DICCON
Yea, in good faith, that is the way,
Fet with some pretty charm.   85
HODGE
Soft, Diccon, be not so hasty yet,
By the mass, for ich begin to sweat –
Cham afraid of some harm!
DICCON
Come hither then, and stir thee not
One inch out of this circle plat,   90
But stand as I thee teach.
HODGE
And shall ich be here safe from their claws?
DICCON
The master devil with his long paws
Here to thee cannot reach.
Now will I settle me to this gear.   95
HODGE
I say, Diccon, hear me, hear:
Go softly to this matter.
DICCON
What devil, man? Art afraid of nought?
HODGE
Canst not tarry a little thought
Till ich make a curtsy of water?   100
DICCON
Stand still to it! Why shouldst thou fear him?

82 *sprite* ed. (spreete Q)
85 *fet* fetched
89 *not* eds (nat Q)
89–90 *stir . . . plat* Diccon presumably draws a circle on the ground.
90 *plat* flat, horizontal
95 *settle . . . gear* get down to business
98 *What . . . nought* Ambiguous. Diccon seems to acknowledge that his conjuration
   is 'nought', nothing. Such subtlety is beyond Hodge's grasp.
99–112 It is clear from the dialogue what effect Hodge's fear at the imminent appearance of the devil is having on his system. The grossness is not entirely gratuitous: it provides Hodge with a compelling reason for changing to his other
   pair of trousers, the ones Gammer Gurton was mending when she lost the
   needle. That he should be wearing those trousers is essential to the dénouement.
100 *make . . . water* urinate a small amount

HODGE
    Gog's sides, Diccon, methink ich hear him!
    And tarry, chall mar all!
DICCON
    The matter is no worse than I told it –
HODGE
    By the mass, cham able no longer to hold it!   105
    Too bad – ich must beray the hall!
DICCON
    Stand to it, Hodge! Stir not, you whoreson!
    What devil, be thine arse-strings bursten?
    Thyself a while but stay!
    The devil – I smell him – will be here anon!   110
HODGE
    Hold him fast, Diccon! Cham gone, cham gone,
    Chill not be at that fray!   [*Exit*]

Act II, Scene ii

DICCON
    Fie, shitten knave, and out upon thee!
    Above all other louts, fie on thee!
    Is not here a cleanly prank?
    But thy matter was no better,
    Nor thy presence here no sweeter;   5
    To fly I can thee thank!
    Here is a matter worthy glozing
    Of Gammer Gurton's needle losing,
    And a foul piece of work.
    A man, I think, might make a play   10
    And need no word to this they say,
    Being but half a clerk.

---

103 *And tarry* If I stay here any longer
106 *beray* dirty, defoul
    the hall Hodge refers to the hall (presumably of Christ's College, Cambridge)
    where the play was performed.

   4, 9 *thy matter; a foul ... work* Sarcastic allusions to Hodge's soiling himself for fear
    of the devil in the preceding scene.
   7 *glozing* glossing, writing a scholarly commentary upon
  10–12 *A man ... clerk* Diccon, commenting on the frantic behaviour of others, for
    which he is in part responsible, says that even a half-educated man could make
    a play about it, without adding anything to what the characters themselves say.
    The author indulges in a metadramatic joke at his own expense.

Soft, let me alone: I will take the charge
This matter further to enlarge
Within a time short.   15
If ye will mark my toys, and note,
I will give ye leave to cut my throat
If I make not good sport! –
Dame Chat, I say, where be ye! Within?
DAME CHAT [*Within her house*]
Who have we there maketh such a din?   20
DICCON
Here is a good fellow, maketh no great danger.
DAME CHAT [*At her doorway*]
What, Diccon? Come near, ye be no stranger.
We be fast set at trump, man, hard by the fire;
Thou shalt set on the king if thou come a little nigher.
DICCON
Nay, nay, there is no tarrying; I must be gone again.   25
But first for you in counsel I have a word or twain.
DAME CHAT
Come hither, Doll! Doll, sit down and play this game,
And as thou sawest me do, see thou do even the same.
There is five trumps beside the queen, the hindmost thou
    shalt find her.
Take heed of Sim Glover's wife – she hath an eye behind
    her!   30

[*Enter* DAME CHAT]

Now, Diccon, say your will.
DICCON   Nay, soft a little yet;
I would not tell it my sister, the matter is so great.

16 *mark my toys* observe my devices
19–31 Location of the action here is uncertain. Dame Chat is in her house and pre-
    sumably invisible to the audience when Diccon calls to her (l. 19). He might
    then approach the doorway, looking into the house at l. 21. Dame Chat's lines
    to Doll (27–30) could be spoken from within, or at the doorway. Tydeman (p.
    238) has Doll appear 'at the door' at l. 27, then go inside at l. 30; Dame Chat
    'appears at the ale-house door' at l. 21 in his edition. Certainly at l. 31 she 'en-
    ters', or comes out of her house. An outstanding example of a character half on
    and half off stage addressing an invisible person within the house (who in fact is
    never seen in the play), occurs in the earliest surviving translation of Terence (c.
    1530), *Terence in English: That Girl from Andros*, ed. Meg Twycross (Lancaster,
    1987), III.ii.
20, 22 s.d. ed.
23 *trump* a card game, also known as ruff

There I will have you swear by our dear Lady of
    Boulogne,
Saint Dunstan and Saint Donnick, with the three kings of
    Cologne,
That ye shall keep it secret.
DAME CHAT   Gog's bread, that will I do!   35
  As secret as mine own thought, by God and the devil too!
DICCON
  Here is Gammer Gurton your neighbour, a sad and heavy
    wight:
  Her goodly fair red cock at home was stole this last night.
DAME CHAT
  Gog's soul! Her cock with the yellow legs that nightly
    crowed so just?
DICCON
  That cock is stolen.
DAME CHAT   What, was he fet out of the hens' roost?   40
DICCON
  I can not tell where the devil he was kept, under key or
    lock,
  But Tib hath tickled in Gammer's ear that you should
    steal the cock.
DAME CHAT
  Have I, strong whore? By bread and salt –
DICCON   Nay, soft, I
    say, be still!
  Say not one word for all this gear.
DAME CHAT   By the mass, that I will!
  I will have the young whore by the head and the old trot
    by the throat!   45
DICCON
  Not one word, Dame Chat, I say, not one word, for my
    coat!

33–4 *Lady of Boulogne . . . three kings of Cologne* Refers to a shrine to the Virgin Mary
    at Boulogne on the French Channel coast; St Dunstan (c. 909–988), Abbot of
    Glastonbury, then Archbishop of Canterbury, influential counsellor to King
    Edgar, and restorer of declining monastic life in England; St Dominic
    (1170–1221), Spanish founder of the Dominican order of friars; the three Magi,
    or Wise Men, whose supposed relics were taken to Germany in 1162 by
    Frederick Barbarossa and are enshrined in Cologne Cathedral. The barrage of
    saints amounts to a mockery of Roman Catholic practice.
34 *Donnick* ed. (Donnyke Q) Dominic
36 *too* eds (two Q)
39 *just* regularly or accurately
44 *for . . . gear* in spite of this accusation

DAME CHAT

    Shall such a beggar's brawl as that, thinkest thou, make
        me a thief?

    The pox light on her whore's sides, a pestilence and a
        mischief! –

    Come out, thou hungry, needy bitch! O, that my nails be
        short!

DICCON

    Gog's bread, woman, hold your peace! [*Aside*] This gear
        will else pass sport!   50

    I would not for an hundred pound this matter should be
        known,

    That I am author of this tale or have abroad it blown. –

    Did ye not swear ye would be ruled, before the tale I told?

    I said ye must all secret keep and ye said sure ye would!

DAME CHAT

    Would you suffer yourself, Diccon, such a sort to revile
        you,   55

    With slanderous words to blot your name and so to defile
        you?

DICCON

    No, Goodwife Chat, I would be loath such drabs should
        blot my name,

    But yet ye must so order all that Diccon bear no blame.

DAME CHAT

    Go to then, what is your rede? Say on your mind; ye shall
        me rule herein.

DICCON

    Godamercy to Dame Chat! In faith, thou must the gear
        begin.   60

    It is twenty pound to a goose turd, my Gammer will not
        tarry,

    But hitherward she comes as fast as her legs can her carry,

    To brawl with you about her cock, for well I heard Tib
        say

---

47 *brawl* offspring, brat

49 *O, that* How unfortunate that. She shouts this line in the direction of Gammer
   Gurton's house.

50–2 *This gear . . . blown* These lines are surely spoken aside. Diccon is unlikely to
   let Chat know that he considers it all 'sport' or that he is the 'author' of this tale.

57 *drabs* sluts

59 *rede* advice

60 *Godamercy to* God have mercy on

61 *It is . . . turd* The odds are . .

The cock was roasted in your house to breakfast
    yesterday,
And when ye had the carcass eaten, the feathers ye out
    flung,   65
And Doll, your maid, the legs she hid a foot deep in the
    dung.

DAME CHAT

O gracious God, my heart it bursts!

DICCON   Well, rule yourself a
    space,
And Gammer Gurton, when she cometh anon into this
    place,
Then to the quean, let's see, tell her your mind and spare
    not;
So shall Diccon blameless be, and then, go to, I care not.   70

DAME CHAT

Then, whore, beware her throat! I can abide no longer.
In faith, old witch, it shall be seen, which of us two be
    stronger,
And, Diccon, but at your request, I would not stay one
    hour.

DICCON

Well, keep it in till she be here, and then out let it pour;
In the meanwhile get you in, and make no words of this.   75
More of this matter within this hour to hear you shall not
    miss.
Because I know you are my friend, hide it I could not,
    doubtless;
Ye know your harm, see ye be wise about your own
    business.
So fare ye well.

DAME CHAT   Nay, soft, Diccon, and drink. What, Doll,
    I say,
Bring here a cup of the best ale, let's see, come quickly
    away!   [*Exit*]   80

69 *quean* harlot, strumpet
69–70 *Tell . . . care not* Say whatever you like to her, so long as you don't implicate
    me.
80 Although there is no stage direction, one assumes that Doll brings a cup of ale
    out to Diccon, who drinks it as he addresses the audience immediately after-
    wards.

Act II, Scene iii

DICCON

Ye see, masters, the one end tapped of this my short
  device;
Now must we broach t'other too, before the smoke arise.
And by the time they have awhile run, I trust ye need not
  crave it,
But look what lieth in both their hearts, ye are like, sure,
  to have it.

[*Enter* HODGE]

HODGE

Yea, Gog's soul, art alive yet! What, Diccon, dare ich
  come?   5

DICCON

A man is well hied to trust to thee! I will say nothing, but
  mum.
But and ye come any nearer, I pray you see all be sweet!

HODGE

Tush, man, is Gammer's nee'le found? That chwould
  gladly weet.

DICCON

She may thank thee it is not found, for if thou had kept
  thy standing,
The devil he would have fet it out, even, Hodge, at thy
  commanding.   10

HODGE

Gog's heart, and could he tell nothing where the nee'le
  might be found?

DICCON

Ye foolish dolt, ye were to seek ere we had got our
  ground!
Therefore his tale so doubtful was that I could not
  perceive it.

---

1 *tapped* opened
2 *before ... arise* before someone gets suspicious
3 *crave* beg to know
6 *well hied* well sped, well served
  I ... mum Proverbial (Tilley W767).
7 *and* if
8 *weet* know
12 *ye were ... ground* you disappeared before we had stationed ourselves in the right
  place
13 *doubtful* obscure

HODGE

Then ich see well something was said; chope one day yet
    to have it.
But Diccon, Diccon, did not the devil cry 'Ho, ho, ho'?   15

DICCON

If thou hadst tarried where thou stoodst, thou wouldest
    have said so.

HODGE

Durst swear of a book, cheard him roar, straight after ich
    was gone!
But tell me, Diccon, what said the knave? Let me hear it
    anon.

DICCON

The whoreson talked to me, I know not well of what:
One while his tongue it ran and paltered of a cat,   20
Another while he stammered still upon a rat,
Last of all there was nothing but every word 'Chat, Chat'.
But this I well perceived before I would him rid:
Between Chat and the rat and the cat the needle is hid.
Now whether Gib our cat have eat it in her maw,   25
Or Doctor Rat our curate have found it in the straw,
Or this Dame Chat your neighbour have stolen it, God he
    knoweth,
But by the morrow at this time, we shall learn how the
    matter goeth.

HODGE

Canst not learn tonight, man? Seest not what is here?

Pointing behind to his torn breeches

14 *chope* I hope
15 *did ... 'Ho, ho, ho'* Traditional cry of the devil, usually upon his entrance, in
    early drama. See, for example, *The Conversion of St Paul* (in *English Moral
    Interludes*, ed. G. Wickham), l. 412 and preceding s.d.: '*Here to enter a devil with
    thunder and fire, and to avaunt himself saying as foloweth ...* : Belial. Ho! ho!
    Behold me, the mighty prince of the parts infernal!'; compare the s.d. '... Devil
    entereth saying "Oh, oh, oh!"' in Thomas Garter's *Susanna* (c. 1569), ll.
    1382–3. As Hodge's query implies, devils are expected to roar; Hodge, despite
    having fled the scene, asserts here (l. 17) and later (III.ii.13) that the devil did
    indeed roar.
17 *Durst ... book* I'd dare to swear on the Bible
    cheard ed. (chard Q) I heard
20 *paltered* mumbled
23 *rid* dispatch
25 *maw* stomach
29 s.d. *Pointing ... breeches* Between his exit at the end of II.i and his entrance near
    the beginning of this scene, Hodge has changed his soiled trousers for the pair
    that Gammer Gurton had begun mending.

DICCON
    'Tis not possible to make it sooner appear.   30
HODGE
    Alas, Diccon, then chave no shift, but, lest ich tarry too
        long,
    Hie me to Sim Glover's shop, there to seek for a thong,
    Therewith this breech to tache and tie as ich may.
DICCON
    Tomorrow, Hodge, if we chance to meet, shalt see what I
        will say.

[*Exit* HODGE]

Act II, Scene iv

DICCON
    Now this gear must forward go, for here my Gammer
        cometh.
    Be still awhile, and say nothing. Make here a little
        roomth.

[*Enter* GAMMER GURTON]

GAMMER GURTON
    Good Lord, shall never be my luck my nee'le again to
        spy?
    Alas the while, 'tis past my help; where 'tis still it must lie.
DICCON
    Now Jesus, Gammer Gurton, what driveth you to this
        sadness?   5
    I fear me, by my conscience, you will sure fall to
        madness!
GAMMER GURTON
    Who is that? What, Diccon? Cham lost, man – fie, fie!
DICCON
    Marry, fie on them that be worthy! But what should be
        your trouble?

---

33 *tache* fasten, secure

1 *Now ... go* Now my plot will advance
2 *Make ... roomth* Diccon instructs spectators to stand aside to let Gammer
    through. See Introduction, p. xxiii.
8 *Marry* (interjection; originally 'Mary', i.e. the Virgin Mary)

GAMMER GURTON

    Alas, the more ich think on it, my sorrow it waxeth
       double.

    My goodly tossing spurrier's nee'le chave lost ich wot not
       where.   10

DICCON

    Your nee'le? When?

GAMMER GURTON   My nee'le, alas! Ich might full ill it
       spare,

    As God himself he knoweth, ne'er one beside chave.

DICCON

    If this be all, good Gammer, I warrant you all is save.

GAMMER GURTON

    Why, know you any tidings which way my nee'le is gone?

DICCON

    Yea, that I do doubtless, as ye shall hear anon: 15

    A' see a thing this matter toucheth within these twenty
       hours,

    Even at this gate before my face, by a neighbour of yours.

    She stooped me down and up she took a needle or a pin –

    I durst be sworn it was even yours, by all my mother's
       kin!

GAMMER GURTON

    It was my nee'le, Diccon, ich wot, for here, even by this
       post,   20

    Ich sat what time as ich up start, and so my nee'le it lost.

    Who was it, lief son? Speak, ich pray thee, and quickly tell
       me that.

DICCON

    A subtle quean as any in this town, your neighbour here,
       Dame Chat.

---

10 *tossing* that moves to and fro quickly in sewing
   spurrier's spur-maker's

12 *ne'er . . . chave* I don't have another one

13 *save* saved

15–23 Diccon's lie and false accusation of Dame Chat here complement his previ-
   ous lie and the implicating of Tib and Gammer Gurton concerning the cock
   (II.ii).

16 *A' see* I've seen

17 *at this gate* Perhaps a wicket gate opening on the street from Gammer Gurton's
   front yard; or simply the house door. The 'post' (l. 20) was mentioned at I.iv.34.

21 *ich sat . . . up start* I was sitting at the time I started up

22 *lief* eds (leive Q) dear

GAMMER GURTON

> Dame Chat, Diccon! Let me be gone, chill thither in post
>   haste!

DICCON

> Take my counsel yet or ye go, for fear ye walk in waste.   25
> It is a murrain crafty drab and froward to be pleased;
> And ye take not the better way, your needle yet ye lose it,
> For when she took it up, even here before your doors,
> 'What, soft, Dame Chat', quoth I 'that same is none of
>   yours'.
> 'Avaunt', quoth she, 'sir knave. What pratest thou of that
>   I find?   30
> I would thou hadst kissed me I wot where!' (she meant, I
>   know, behind);
> And home she went as brag as it had been a body-louse,
> And I after, as bold as it had been the goodman of the
>   house.
> But there and ye had heard her, how she began to scold!
> The tongue it went on pattens, by him that Judas sold!   35
> Each other word I was a knave and you a whore of
>   whores,
> Because I spoke in your behalf and said the nee'le was
>   yours.

GAMMER GURTON

> Gog's bread, and thinks the callet thus to keep my nee'le
>   me fro?

DICCON

> Let her alone and she minds none other but even to dress
>   you so.

GAMMER GURTON

> By the mass, chill rather spend the coat that is on my
>   back!   40

---

25 *or* before
26 *murrain* cursed
   froward . . . pleased hard to please
27 *lose* Q (some eds emend to *lese* to restore rhyme with *pleased*)
29 *soft* not so hasty
30 *Avaunt* Begone
32 *brag* saucily
   as it as if she
33 *goodman* master
35 *went on pattens* made a great clatter
38 *callet* lewd woman, scold
   fro from
39 *Let . . . so* You may be sure that she intends to do exactly that to you

Thinks the false quean by such a slight that chill my
    nee'le lack?

DICCON

Sleep not your gear, I counsel you, but of this take good
    heed:

Let not be known I told you of it, how well soever ye
    speed.

GAMMER GURTON

Chill in, Diccon, a clean apron to take and set before me;

And ich may my nee'le once see, chill sure remember
    thee!   [*Exit*]   45

Act II, Scene v

DICCON

Here will the sport begin, if these two once may meet;
Their cheer, durst lay money, will prove scarcely sweet!
My Gammer sure intends to be upon her bones
With staves or with clubs or else with cobblestones!
Dame Chat, on the other side, if she be far behind   5
I am right far deceived; she is given to it of kind.
He that may tarry by it awhile, and that but short,
I warrant him, trust to it, he shall see all the sport.
Into the town will I, my friends to visit there,
And hither straight again to see th' end of this gear.   10
[*To the musicians*] In the meantime, fellows, pipe up your
    fiddles; I say, take them,
And let your friends hear such mirth as ye can make
    them.   [*Exit*]

---

42 *Sleep . . . gear* Do not neglect this matter

Act II, Scene v This 'scene' is merely the introduction to a musical interlude, and the
    occasion for Diccon to whet the audience's appetite for what is to follow.
  6 *given . . . kind* naturally disposed to violent abuse
11 *pipe . . . fiddles* strike up the music. The musicians would most likely have been
    stationed in the gallery, above the playing area, at the screens end of the college
    hall.

Act III, Scene i

[*Enter* HODGE]

HODGE

Sim Glover, yet gramercy! Cham meetly well sped now;
Th'art even as good a fellow as ever kissed a cow!
Here is a thong indeed, by the mass, though ich speak it –
Tom Tankard's great bald curtal, I think, could not break
    it!
And when he spied my need to be so straight and hard,   5
H'as lent me here his nawl to set the jib forward.
As for my Gammer's nee'le, the flying fiend go weet,
Chill not now go to the door again with it to meet!
Chwould make shift good enough, and chad a candle's
    end;
The chief hole in my breech with these two chill amend.   10

Act III, Scene ii

[*Enter* GAMMER GURTON]

GAMMER GURTON

Now Hodge, mayst now be glad, cha' news to tell thee:
Ich know who has my nee'le; ich trust soon shalt it see.

HODGE

The devil thou does! Hast heard, Gammer, indeed, or
    dost but jest?

GAMMER GURTON

'Tis as true as steel, Hodge.

HODGE   Why, knowest well where
    didst lose it?

1 *gramercy* God grant you mercy
  meetly . . . sped well provided for
3 *thong* eds. (thynge Q)
4 *bald curtal* piebald horse with a docked tail
5 *straight* urgent
6 *H'as* (Hays Q) He has   *nawl* awl   *set . . . forward* hasten matters on
  jib (gyb Q) forward-most triangular sail in certain systems of ship's rigging
7 *the flying . . . weet* the devil take it
9 *candle's end* a small piece of candle. Another of the several indications that it is
  dusk or evening in the fictional day of the play's action, as it certainly was also
  at its actual time of performance.
10 *these two* (i.e., the awl and thong)

4 *lose* ed. (leese Q)

GAMMER GURTON
    Ich know who found it and took it up; shalt see, or it be
        long.   5
HODGE
    God's mother dear! If that be true, farewell both nawl and
        thong!
    But who has it, Gammer? Say on, chwould fain hear it
        disclosed.
GAMMER GURTON
    That false vixen, that same Dame Chat, that counts
        herself so honest!
HODGE
    Who told you so?
GAMMER GURTON   That same did Diccon the bedlam,
        which saw it done.
HODGE
    Diccon? It is a vengeable knave, Gammer, 'tis a bonable
        whoreson,   10
    Can do mo' things than that, else cham deceived evil.
    By the mass, ich saw him of late call up a great black
        devil!
    'O!' the knave cried, 'Ho, ho!' He roared and he
        thundered!
    And ye 'ad been here, cham sure you'ld murrainly ha'
        wondered.
GAMMER GURTON
    Was not thou afraid, Hodge, to see him in this place?   15
HODGE
    No, and he 'ad come to me, chwould have laid him on
        the face,
    Chwould have, promised him.
GAMMER GURTON   But Hodge, had he no
        horns to push?

---

   5 *or* before
10–11 *It is . . . evil* It would be a very great scoundrel indeed who could do more
    (villainous) things than Diccon, or I'm badly mistaken.
10 *vengeable* vengeful (here, perhaps, simply 'very great')
    bonable abominable
11 *mo'* ed. (mo Q) more
12–26 Hodge's ready imagination reconstructs an event that never occurred.
14 *murrainly ha' wondered* been mightily astonished
16 *he 'ad* ed. (chad Q)
16, 17, 21 *chwould* ed. (chould Q)
16 Hodge's bravery is after the fact; compare his behaviour at II.i.86–112.

HODGE
    As long as your two arms! Saw ye never Friar Rush
    Painted on a cloth, with a sidelong cow's tale,
    And crooked cloven feet and many a hooked nail?   20
    For all the world, if I should judge, chwould reckon him
      his brother;
    Look, even what face Friar Rush had, the devil had such
      another!
GAMMER GURTON
    Now Jesus mercy, Hodge! Did Diccon in him bring?
HODGE
    Nay, Gammer, hear me speak; chill tell you a greater
      thing.
    The devil, when Diccon bad him (ich heard him
      wondrous well)   25
    Said plainly here before us, that Dame Chat had your
      nee'le.

        [DAME CHAT *appears at the door of her house*]

GAMMER GURTON
    Then let us go and ask her wherefore she minds to keep
      it;
    Seeing we know so much, 'twere a madness now to sleep
      it.
HODGE
    Go to her, Gammer. See ye not where she stands in her
      doors?
    Bid her give you the nee'le; 'tis none of hers, but yours.   30

18–22 The Friar Rush legend was of Danish origin, popular in Germany, and ob-
    viously familiar in England by the mid-16th century, although the earliest extant
    English version dates from 1620. Rush was a devil, sent by Satan to create havoc
    among the friars. Later he became a mischievous spirit generally, like Puck or
    Robin Goodfellow. He is the main character in Thomas Dekker's play, *If it be
    not good, the Devil is in it* (c. 1611).
25–6 Hodge repeats what Diccon, not the devil, has said (II.iii.19–27).
25 *bad* commanded
26 s.d. Tydeman. Justified by l. 29.
28 *sleep it* ignore, neglect it
29 *See . . . doors* Dame Chat would have appeared at her door at some point during
    the scene, drawn (if explanation is needed) by the sound of Gammer's voice out-
    side; she has been eagerly awaiting her since II.ii.

Act III, Scene iii

GAMMER GURTON

    Dame Chat, chwould pray thee fair, let me have that is
        mine!

    Chill not this twenty years take one fart that is thine;

    Therefore give me mine own, and let me live beside thee.

DAME CHAT

    Why art thou crept from home hither to mine own doors
        to chide me?

    Hence, doting drab, avaunt, or I shall set thee further!   5

    Intends thou and that knave me in my house to murder?

GAMMER GURTON

    Tush, gape not so on me, woman! Shalt not yet eat me,

    Nor all the friends thou hast in this shall not entreat me.

    Mine own goods I will have, and ask thee no by-leave.

    What, woman? Poor folks must have right, though the
        thing you agrieve.   10

DAME CHAT

    Give thee thy right and hang thee up, with all thy beggar's
        brood!

    What, wilt thou make me a thief, and say I stole thy good?

GAMMER GURTON

    Chill say nothing, ich warrant thee, but that ich can prove
        it well:

    Thou fet my good even from my door, cham able this to
        tell.

DAME CHAT

    Did I, old witch, steal aught was thine? How should that
        thing be known?   15

Act III, Scene iii Throughout this scene, the play's centrepiece, neither woman names
    the object in question, which Dame Chat thinks is the cock and Gammer, her
    needle. It is, of course, Diccon's doing that they are at such utter cross-purposes.

  1 *chwould* ed. (cholde Q)

  5 *doting* foolish

  6 *murder* ed. (murther Q)

  7 *on me, woman* eds (no me Woman Q; no, woman 1661)

  9 *no by-leave* Boas (on beleve Q)

    and . . . by-leave without asking your permission

 12 *good* goods, property

 15 *aught* ed. (oft. Q) anything

GAMMER GURTON
   Ich cannot tell, but up thou tookst it as though it had
        been thine own.
DAME CHAT
   Marry, fie on thee, thou old gib, with all my very heart!
GAMMER GURTON
   Nay, fie on thee, thou ramp, thou rig, with all that take
        thy part!
DAME CHAT
   A vengeance on those lips that layeth such things to my
        charge!
GAMMER GURTON
   A vengeance on those callet's hips, whose conscience is
        so large!   20
DAME CHAT
   Come out, hog!
GAMMER GURTON   Come out, hog, and let me have right!
DAME CHAT
   Thou arrant witch!
GAMMER GURTON   Thou bawdy bitch, chill make thee
        curse this night!
DAME CHAT
   A bag and a wallet!
GAMMER GURTON   A cart for a callet!
DAME CHAT   Why, weenest thou
        thus to prevail?
   I hold thee a groat, I shall patch thy coat!
GAMMER GURTON   Thou wert as
        good kiss my tail!

17 *gib* cat (disparagingly, an old woman)
18 *ramp* vulgar woman
   rig wanton woman
20 *callet* lewd woman
21 *Come out* It does not make sense for Chat, who is standing in the doorway of her
   house, literally to say 'Come out' to Gammer, who is outside already (ll. 4, 6).
   The sense is rather that of 'calling someone out', i.e., challenging to a duel, or
   simply 'Come on'.
   hog eds. (Hogge ... hogge Q; not 'Hodge' as a few eds. have it)
   let me have eds (let have me Q)
22 *arrant* notorious
23 *bag ... wallet ... cart* Dame Chat doubtless uses 'wallet' in the special sense of
   a beggar's bag, and Gammer Gurton alludes to the punishment of lewd
   women by tying them to the tailgate of a cart and whipping them through the
   town.
24 *hold* wager

Thou slut, thou cut, thou rakes, thou jakes, will not
    shame make thee hide?   25
DAME CHAT
Thou scald, thou bald, thou rotten, thou glutton, I will no
    longer chide,
But I will teach thee to keep home!
GAMMER GURTON   Wilt thou, drunken
    beast?

[They fight]

HODGE
Stick to her, Gammer, take her by the head! Chill warrant
    you this feast!
Smite, I say, Gammer! Bite, I say, Gammer! I trow ye will
    be keen!
Where be your nails? Claw her by the jaws, pull me out
    both her eyen!   30
Gog's bones, Gammer, hold up your head!
DAME CHAT   I trow, drab, I
    shall dress thee!
[*To* HODGE] Tarry, thou knave! I hold thee a groat, I shall
    make these hands bless thee!

[Exit HODGE *into* GAMMER GURTON's *house]*

25 *cut* horse. Also, phonetically and metaphorically, as crude term of abuse for a
woman, = *cunt* (*OED, cut,* sb. 20: 'a passage or channel ... a natural narrow
opening ... by water'); compare *The Woman Taken in Adultery* in the *N-town*
cycle (late 15th c.), ll. 149–52: 'Come forth, thou quene, com forth, thou
scolde!/ Come forth, thou sloveyn, come forth, thou slutte!/ We shal thee teche,
with carys colde,/ A lityl bettyr to kepe thy kutte' (*Medieval Drama,* ed. D.
Bevington (Boston, 1975), p. 465).
    rakes vague term of abuse, used here merely for rhyme
    jakes privy, toilet
25–6 *hide/ ... chide* Adams (hide/ ... chide thee Q, 1661; some eds supply 'thee' in
l. 25 and retain 'thee' in l. 26)
26 *scald* term of abuse, from a scabby disease of the scalp
28 *Chill ... feast* I'll back you to win this event
28–49 The main movements in the action of this scene can easily be inferred from
the dialogue. Hodge obviously stands well away from the fray, urging Gammer
on (ll. 28–31). She appears to be getting the worst of it, and he runs into the
house to get a weapon (32–4), but despite his brave words (35–40), retreats
quickly once again; the last part of l. 41 would be spoken from within the house.
Between ll. 39 and 42, Doll has brought out a spit, with which Dame Chat
threatens Hodge (42). Gammer takes advantage of this momentary diversion to
grab Dame Chat from behind, but loses her hold and suffers a defiant parting
blow (49).
30 *eyen* eyes

Take thou this, old whore, for amends, and learn thy
   tongue well to tame,
And say thou met at this bickering, not thy fellow but thy
   dame!

[Enter HODGE *with a staff]*

HODGE
Where is the strong-stewed whore? Chill gi'er a whore's
   mark!   35
[*To the audience*] Stand out one's way, that ich kill none in
   the dark! –
Up, Gammer, and ye be alive! Chill fight now for us both!
Come no near me, thou scald callet! To kill thee ich were
   loath!
DAME CHAT
Art here again, thou hoddypeak? What, Doll, bring me
   out my spit!
HODGE
Chill broach thee with this, by m' father's soul! Chill
   conjure that foul sprite!   40

[COCK *appears at the door of* GAMMER'*s house*]

Let door stand, Cock! [*To* DAME CHAT] Why, comes
   indeed? – Keep door, thou whoreson boy!
DAME CHAT
Stand to it, thou dastard, for thine ears! I s' teach thee a
   sluttish toy!
HODGE
Gog's wounds, whore, chill make thee avaunt! Take heed,
   Cock! Pull in the latch!   [*Exit*]
DAME CHAT
I'faith, Sir Loose-Breech, had ye tarried, ye should have
   found your match!

34 *bickering* skirmish, altercation
   not ... dame not your equal but your superior
35 *strong-stewed* belonging to the stews, or brothel
   gi'er ed. (geare Q) give her
38 *near* nearer
39 *hoddypeak* simpleton, blockhead
42 *dastard* coward
   I s' ed. (Ise Q) I shall
   thee a Q (thee, a eds)
   toy trick
44 *Loose-Breech* alluding to Hodge's torn trousers

GAMMER GURTON
Now 'ware thy throat, losel, thou s' pay for all!
HODGE [*From the doorway*]   Well said,
    Gammer, by my soul!   45
  Hoise her! Souse her! Bounce her! Trounce her! Pull out
    her throat-boll!
DAME CHAT
  Comst behind me, thou withered witch! And I get once
    on foot,
  Thou s' pay for all, thou old tarleather! I'll teach thee
    what 'longs to it!
  Take thou this to make up thy mouth, till time thou come
    by more!   [*Exit*]
HODGE [*Coming out*]
  Up, Gammer, stand on your feet! Where is the old
    whore?   50
  Faith, would chad her by the face, chwould crack her
    callet crown!
GAMMER GURTON
  Ah, Hodge, Hodge, where was thy help when vixen had
    me down?
HODGE
  By the mass, Gammer, but for my staff, Chat had gone
    nigh to spill you!
  Ich think the harlot had not cared, and chad not come, to
    kill you!
  But shall we lose our nee'le thus?
GAMMER GURTON   No, Hodge, chwere
    loath do so.   55
  Thinkest thou chill take that at her hand? No, Hodge, ich
    tell thee, no!

---

45 *losel* worthless person
  thou s' ed. (thouse Q) thou shalt
  pay eds (pray Q)
46 *Hoise* 1661 (Hoyse Q; House Boas) raise, hoist ('house' is a variant form of the
  same word)
  souse beat severely
  throat-boll Adam's apple
48 *tarleather* strip of sheepskin used to make thongs (here, a term of abuse)
  teach . . . it show you what's what
53 *spill* kill
55 *chwere* ed. (chwarde Q)

HODGE

> Chwould yet this fray were well take up and our own
>   nee'le at home;
> 'Twill be my chance else some to kill, wherever it be or
>   whom!

GAMMER GURTON

> We have a parson, Hodge, thou knows, a man esteemed
>   wise,
> Mast' Doctor Rat; chill for him send and let me hear his
>   advice.   60
> He will her shrive for all this gear, and give her penance
>   strait;
> We s' have our nee'le, else Dame Chat comes ne'er
>   within heaven gate!

HODGE

> Yea, marry, Gammer, that ich think best. Will you now
>   for him send?
> The sooner Doctor Rat be here, the sooner we s' ha' an
>   end;
> And hear, Gammer! Diccon's devil, as ich remember
>   well,   65
> Of Cat and Chat and Doctor Rat a felonious tale did tell;
> Chold you forty pound that is the way your nee'le to get
>   again.

GAMMER GURTON

> Chill ha' him straight! Call out the boy, we s' make him
>   take the pain.

HODGE

> What, Cock, I say! Come out! What devil, canst not hear?

COCK [*Within*]

> How now, Hodge? How does Gammer! Is yet the
>   weather clear?   70

57 *take up* concluded
60 *Mast'* Master
61 *shrive* hear confession and impose penance
     strait strict
62 *We s'* ed. (Wese Q) we shall
65 *hear* eds (here Q)
67 *Chold* I hold, wager
68 *straight* straightaway
70 s.p. COCK eds (GAMMER Q)

What would sh'ave me to do?
GAMMER GURTON   Come hither, Cock, anon!

[*Enter* COCK]

Hence swith to Doctor Rat! Hie thee that thou were gone,
And pray him come speak with me; cham not well at
    ease.
Shalt have him at his chamber, or else at Mother Bee's,
Else seek him at Hob Filcher's shop, for as cheard it
    reported,   75
There is the best ale in all the town, and now is most
    resorted.
COCK
And shall ich bring him with me, Gammer?
GAMMER GURTON   Yea, by and
    by, good Cock.
COCK
Shalt see that shall be here anon, else let me have on the
    dock!   [*Exit*]
HODGE
Now, Gammer, shall we two go in and tarry for his
    coming?
What devil, woman! Pluck up your heart, and leave off
    all this glumming.   80
Though she were stronger at the first, as ich think ye did
    find her,
Yet there ye dressed the drunken sow, what time ye came
    behind her.
GAMMER GURTON
Nay, nay, cham sure she lost not all, for set th' end to the
    beginning,
And ich doubt not but she will make small boast of her
    winning.

71 *sh'ave* ed. (chave Q)
71 s.d. *Enter* COCK ed. (after l. 69 eds)
72 *swith* quickly
75 *cheard* ed. (charde Q)
76 *resorted* frequented
78 *dock* buttocks
80 *glumming* being glum or dejected
83-4 Hodge has reminded Gammer of how she jumped upon Chat from behind,
    while Gammer recalls the parting blow she received from Chat afterwards (l. 49)
    and is sure Chat will claim victory; 'small' is ironic.

Act III, Scene iv

[Enter TIB *with* GIB *the cat]*

TIB

    See, Gammer, Gammer! Gib, our cat, cham afraid what
        she aileth!

    She stands me gasping behind the door, as though her
        wind her faileth.

    Now let ich doubt what Gib should mean, that now she
        doth so dote.

HODGE

    Hold hither! Ich hold twenty pound your nee'le is in her
        throat!

    Grope her, ich say! Methinks ich feel it. Does not prick
        your hand?   5

GAMMER GURTON

    Ich can feel nothing.

HODGE   No, ich know there's not within this
        land

    A murrainer cat than Gib is, betwixt the Thames and
        Tyne;

    Sh'as as much wit in her head almost as chave in mine!

TIB

    Faith, sh'as eaten something that will not easily down;

    Whether she got it at home or abroad in the town,   10

    Ich cannot tell.

GAMMER GURTON Alas, ich fear it be some crooked pin!

    And then farewell, Gib! She is undone and lost all save
        the skin.

HODGE

    'Tis your nee'le, woman, I say! Gog's soul, give me a
        knife,

    And chill have it out of her maw, or else chall lose my life!

---

2 *me* (used here as an expletive; the ethical dative)

3 *Now ... doubt* 'Let' should perhaps be 'yet' (or 'mot' [= must] as Hazlitt conjectured); or 'ich' be amended to 'mich' or 'me'. But Q's version may be intentional, reflecting Tib's tenuous command of grammar.
  doth so dote appears out of her wits

4 *Hold hither* Hand her to me
  Ich hold ed. (ichould Q) I wager

7 *murrainer* more cursed

8 *Sh'as* ed. (Shase Q) she has

12 *all save* except

13 *'Tis* eds (Tyb Q)

GAMMER GURTON
　　What? Nay, Hodge, fie! Kill not our cat! 'Tis all the cats
　　　　we ha' now!   15
HODGE
　　By the mass, Dame Chat has me so moved, ich care not
　　　　what I kill, ma' God a vow!
　　Go to then, Tib, to this gear! Hold up her tail and take
　　　　her!
　　Chill see what devil is in her guts! Chill take the pains to
　　　　rake her!
GAMMER GURTON
　　Rake a cat, Hodge? What wouldst thou do?
HODGE   What,
　　　　thinkst that cham not able?
　　Did not Tom Tankard rake his curtal t'other day,
　　　　standing in the stable?   20

                        [*Enter* COCK]

GAMMER GURTON
　　Soft, be content. Let's hear what news Cock bringeth
　　　　from Mast' Rat.
COCK
　　Gammer, chave been there as you bad, you wot well
　　　　about what;
　　'Twill not be long before he come, ich durst swear of a
　　　　book.
　　He bids you see ye be at home, and there for him to look.
GAMMER GURTON
　　Where didst thou find him, boy? Was he not where I told
　　　　thee?   25
COCK
　　Yes, yes, even at Hob Filcher's house, by him that bought
　　　　and sold me!
　　A cup of ale had in his hand, and a crab lay in the fire.
　　Chad much ado to go and come, all was so full of mire.
　　And Gammer, one thing I can tell; Hob Filcher's nawl
　　　　was lost,

---

16 *ma'* I make
18 *rake* A term from farriery: 'to clean (a costive horse or its fundament) from or-
　　dure by scraping with the hand' (*OED*).
20 *t'other* ed. (toore Q)
23 *of a book* on the Bible
26 *him . . . me* Christ
29 *nawl* awl

And Doctor Rat found it again, hard beside the door
    post. 30
Ich hold a penny can say something your nee'le again to
    fet.

GAMMER GURTON

Cham glad to hear so much, Cock. Then trust he will not
    let
To help us herein best he can; therefore till time he come,
Let us go in. If there be aught to get thou shalt have
    some.

[*Exeunt*]

Act [IV], Scene [i]

[*Enter* DOCTOR RAT]

DOCTOR RAT

A man were better twenty times be a bandog and bark,
Than here among such a sort be parish priest or clerk,
Where he shall never be at rest one pissing-while a day,
But he must trudge about the town, this way and that
    way;
Here to a drab, there to a thief, his shoes to tear and rent, 5
And that which is worst of all, at every knave's
    commandment!
I had not sit the space to drink two pots of ale
But Gammer Gurton's sorry boy was straightway at my
    tail,
And she was sick and I must come, to do I wot not what.
If once her finger's end but ache, 'Trudge! Call for
    Doctor Rat!' 10
And when I come not at their call, I only thereby lose,

31 *can* he can
32 *let* neglect, fail
34 *aught to get* any food to eat

Act IV, Scene i eds. (The ii Acte. The iiii. Sceane. Q, 1661)
    1 *bandog* Originally, a dog kept chained because of its ferocity; here, simply a dog.
    5 *his shoes* (the priest's not the thief's)
    7 *sit the space* been sitting long enough
    10 *Trudge* Go quickly

For I am sure to lack therefore a tithe-pig or a goose.
I warrant you, when truth is known, and told they have
    their tale,
The matter whereabout I came is not worth a
    halfpennyworth of ale!
Yet must I talk so sage and smooth as though I were a
    glozer,   15
Else or the year come at an end, I shall be, sure, the loser.
[*At* GAMMER GURTON's *door*] What work ye, Gammer
    Gurton? Ho! Here is your friend, Master Rat.

[*Enter* GAMMER GURTON]

GAMMER GURTON
Ah, good master Doctor, cha' troubled, cha' troubled
    you, chwot well that!
DOCTOR RAT
How do ye, woman? Be ye lusty, or be ye not well at ease?
GAMMER GURTON
By gis, master, cham not sick, but yet chave a disease.   20
Chad a foul turn now of late; chill tell it you, by gigs!
DOCTOR RAT
Hath your brown cow cast her calf or your sandy sow her
    pigs?
GAMMER GURTON
No, but chad been as good they had, as this, ich wot well.
DOCTOR RAT
What is the matter?

12 *tithe-pig ... goose* Donations from parishioners to the priest, upon which he de-
pended to supplement his meagre salary. Specifically, the tithe was one-tenth of
goods or wealth, to be given to the church for the maintenance of religion.
Scriptural authority is found in the Old Testament (e.g., Leviticus 27:30,
Deuteronomy 14:22, Malachi 3:10), and tithing was enforced by law in England
as early as 900. As vicar, Dr Rat would have to collect the 'small' tithe (small
animals, fruit, vegetables) himself, the 'large' tithe of the major crops going to
the rector or incumbent, probably the bishop or a monastery (or, after the dis-
solution of monasteries in the 1530s, a lay rector). Hence his concern to remain
on good terms with his parishioners.
15 *glozer* ed. (glosier Q) flatterer
16 *or* before
17 *What ... ye* What are you doing
   Ho! ed. (hoow Q; How? eds)
19 *lusty* in good health
20, 21 *gis; gigs* Jesus
22 *cast* given birth prematurely

GAMMER GURTON   Alas, alas, cha' lost my good nee'le!
　My nee'le, I say, and wot ye what? A drab came by and
　　spied it,   25
　And when I asked her for the same, the filth flatly denied
　　it!
DOCTOR RAT
　What was she that –
GAMMER GURTON   A dame, ich warrant you! She began
　　to scold and brawl –
　Alas, Alas! [*Calling into the house*] Come hither, Hodge!
　[*To* DOCTOR RAT] This wretch can tell you all.

Act IV, Scene ii

[*Enter* HODGE]

HODGE
　Good morrow, Gaffer Vicar!
DOCTOR RAT   Come on, fellow, let us hear.
　Thy dame hath said to me thou knowest of all this gear;
　Let's see what thou canst say.
HODGE   By m' fay, sir, that ye shall!
　What matter soever here was done, ich can tell your
　　ma'ship all.
　　My Gammer Gurton here, see now,   5
　　　sat her down at this door, see now;
　　And as she began to stir her, see now,
　　　her nee'le fell in the floor, see now;
　　And while her staff she took, see now,
　　　at Gib her cat to fling, see now,   10
　　Her nee'le was lost in the floor, see now –
　　　Is not this a wondrous thing, see now?
　　Then came the quean, Dame Chat, see now,
　　　to ask for her black cup, see now,
　　And even here at this gate, see now,   15
　　　she took that nee'le up, see now.

---

　1 *Gaffer* Contraction of 'godfather' or 'grandfather'; the masculine form of 'gam-
　　mer'. Apparently applied originally by country people to elderly persons or those
　　entitled to respect. The earliest recorded occurrences of both forms are in this
　　play.
　3 *fay* faith
　4 *all* eds (not in Q, 1661)
　5–28 These lines are set thus in Q
　14 *to . . . cup* This new detail is the product of Hodge's imagination, embroidering
　　upon the original hint supplied by Diccon (II.iv.16–37).

My Gammer then she yede, see now,
   her nee'le again to bring, see now,
And was caught by the head, see now –
   Is not this a wondrous thing, see now?   20
She tare my Gammer's coat, see now,
   and scratched her by the face, see now;
Chad thought sh'ad stopped her throat, see now –
   Is not this a wondrous case, see now?
When ich saw this, ich was wroth, see now,   25
   and start between them twain, see now;
Else ich durst take a book oath, see now,
   my Gammer had been slain, see now!

GAMMER GURTON

This is even the whole matter, as Hodge has plainly told,
And chwould fain be quiet for my part, that chwould.   30
But help us, good master, beseech ye that ye do,
Else shall we both be beaten and lose our nee'le too.

DOCTOR RAT

What would ye have me to do? Tell me that I were gone;
I will do the best that I can, to set you both at one.
But be ye sure Dame Chat hath this your nee'le found?   35

[*Enter* DICCON]

GAMMER GURTON

Here comes the man that see her take it up off the
   ground;
Ask him yourself, Master Rat, if ye believe not me,
And help me to my nee'le, for God's sake and Saint
   Charity!

---

17 *yede* went   21 *tare* tore
25 *wroth* angry   26 *start* went
33 *that . . . gone* so that I may go do it
34 *set . . . one* make peace between you
35 s.d. Enter DICCON Boas (after l. 39 eds)
38 *Saint Charity* eds (saint charitie Q) Q's small letters may mean that no proper
   names is intended; 'saint' would mean 'holy'. However, such usage, as proper
   names, was current until the seventeenth century (e.g., Saint Cross, Saint Spirit,
   Saint Trinity; compare 'By Gis and by Saint Charity', *Hamlet* IV.v.56). There
   were said to be three sisters, Saints Faith, Hope and Charity, martyred in Rome
   under the emperor Hadrian, but 'the concatenation of names is itself suspicious'
   (Donald Attwater, *A Dictionary of Saints* [1965], p. 127). The tradition was well
   established by the tenth century, when the three (Fides, Spes, Caritas) figured
   as dramatic characters, the holy daughters of Wisdom, in a Latin play, *Sapientia*,
   by a German nun, Hrotsvitha (or Roswitha). See *The Plays of Roswitha*, trans. C.
   St John (1923), pp. 131–58.

DOCTOR RAT
   Come near, Diccon, and let us hear what thou can
      express.
   Wilt thou be sworn thou seest Dame Chat this woman's
      nee'le have?   40
DICCON
   Nay, by Saint Benit, will I not! Then might ye think me
      rave!
GAMMER GURTON
   Why, didst not thou tell me so even here? Canst thou for
      shame deny it?
DICCON
   Ay, marry, Gammer, but I said I would not abide by it.
DOCTOR RAT
   Will you say a thing and not stick to it to try it?
DICCON
   'Stick to it', quoth you, Master Rat? Marry, sir, I defy it!   45
   Nay, there is many an honest man, when he such blasts
      hath blown
   In his friends' ears, he would be loath the same by him
      were known.
   If such a toy be used oft among the honesty,
   It may beseem a simple man, of your and my degree.
DOCTOR RAT
   Then we be never the nearer, for all that you can tell!   50
DICCON
   Yes, marry, sir, if ye will do by mine advice and counsel.
   If Mother Chat see all us here, she knoweth how the
      matter goes.
   Therefore I rede you three go hence, and within keep
      close,
   And I will into Dame Chat's house, and so the matter
      use,
   That or you could go twice to church, I warrant you hear
      news.   55
   She shall look well about her, but I durst lay a pledge,

41 *Saint Benit* St. Benedict, sixth-century founder of the monastic movement.
   think me rave believe me to be mad
43 He did so at II.iv.43.
44 *try* prove
47 *the same ... known* that it were known to come from him
48 *honesty* honourable people
49 *beseem* be fitting for
53 *rede* advise

Ye shall of Gammer's nee'le have shortly better
    knowledge.

GAMMER GURTON

Now, gentle Diccon, do so, and good sir, let us trudge.

DOCTOR RAT

By the mass, I may not tarry so long to be your judge!

DICCON

'Tis but a little while, man! What, take so much pain!   60
If I hear no news of it, I will come sooner again.

HODGE

Tarry so much, good Master Doctor, of your gentleness.

DOCTOR RAT

Then let us hie us inward and, Diccon, speed thy
    business.

                                    [*Exeunt except* DICCON]

[Act IV, Scene iii]

DICCON [*To the audience*]

Now, sirs, do you no more but keep my counsel just,
And Doctor Rat shall thus catch some good, I trust.
But Mother Chat, my gossip, talk first withal I must,
For she must be chief captain to lay the Rat in the dust.

                     [*Enter* DAME CHAT]

Good even, Dame Chat, in faith, and well met in this
    place.   5

DAME CHAT

Good even, my friend Diccon. Whither walk ye this pace?

DICCON

By my truth, even to you, to learn how the world goeth.

---

60 *take . . . pain* put yourself to this slight inconvenience

Act IV, Scene iii There is no scene division here in Q, but based on its practice hereto-
    fore a new scene should begin here, and most eds introduce one. In Q, scene ii
    continues to the end of Act IV.
  1 *do . . . just* if you will only keep my secret
  4 s.d. *Enter* DAME CHAT eds
  5, 6 *Good even* Boas (God deven Q). Q's 'God deven' probably represents a con-
    traction of 'God give you good even', and some editors retain it.
  6 *this pace* at such a pace

Heard ye no more of the other matter? Say me now, by
    your troth.

DAME CHAT

Oh yes, Diccon! Here the old whore and Hodge, that
    great knave –
But, in faith, I would thou hadst seen! O Lord, I dressed
    them brave!   10
She bare me two or three souses behind in the nape of the
    neck,
Till I made her old weasand to answer again, 'Keck!'
And Hodge, that dirty dastard, that at her elbow stands,
If one pair of legs had not been worth two pair of hands,
He had had his beard shaven, if my nails would have
    served,   15
And not without a cause, for the knave it well deserved!

DICCON

By the mass, I can thee thank, wench, thou didst so well
    acquit thee!

DAME CHAT

And th'adst seen him, Diccon, it would have made thee
    beshit thee
For laughter. The whoreson dolt at last caught up a club,
As though be would have slain the master devil
    Beelzebub;   20
But I set him soon inward.

DICCON   O Lord, there is the thing
That Hodge is so offended, that makes him start and
    fling!

DAME CHAT

Why? Makes the knave any moiling, as ye have seen or
    heard?

DICCON

Even now I saw him last, like a madman he fared,
And sware by heaven and hell he would awreak his
    sorrow,   25

---

10 *dressed . . . brave* beat them soundly
11 *bare* bore, gave
   souses blows
12 *weasand* windpipe
13 *dastard* coward
14 *If . . . hands* If Hodge had not been so quick on his legs (in running away)
21 *thing* reason
23 *makes . . . moiling* is he raving
25 *sware* swore
   awreak be avenged for

And leave you never a hen on live by eight of the clock
    tomorrow.
Therefore mark what I say and my words see that ye
    trust:
Your hens be as good as dead if you leave them on the
    roost.

DAME CHAT
The knave dare as well go hang himself as go upon my
    ground!

DICCON
Well, yet take heed, I say; I must tell you my tale round.   30
Have you not about your house, behind your furnace or
    lead,
A hole where a crafty knave may creep in for need?

DAME CHAT
Yes, by the mass, a hole broke down, even within these
    two days.

DICCON
Hodge, he intends this same night, to slip in there aways.

DAME CHAT
O Christ, that I were sure of it! In faith, he should have
    his meed!   35

DICCON
Watch well, for the knave will be there, as sure as is your creed!
I would spend myself a shilling to have him swinged well.

DAME CHAT
I am as glad as a woman can be, of this thing to hear tell!
By Gog's bones, when he cometh, now that I know the
    matter,

---

26 *on live* alive

30 *tell . . . round* finish my story

31 *furnace* oven

    lead Most eds describe as a large pot or cauldron, made of lead, often used for
brewing. See, however, Southern, pp. 407–8 for the suggestion that the lead
(rhymes with 'need') may have been a sort of smoke-conduit cut through the
wall of the house from the back of the fireplace to the outside, a feature report-
edly present in some Tudor cottages. But *OED* gives no examples of such a
usage. Diccon asks about a hole *behind* the furnace or lead, and Chat's reply (l.
33) seems to imply that it is not a regular architectural feature of her house.
Though Southern's conjecture is plausible, Dame Chat would, as an alewife,
have such a large cauldron for brewing, in or near her furnace or fireplace; see
Doctor Rat's allusion to a swill tub at IV.iv.35, and to 'the back hole' at V.ii.189.

35 *meed* reward

36 *creed* religious faith

37 *swinged* thrashed

He shall sure at the first skip to leap in scalding water,   40
With a worse turn besides. When he will, let him come!

DICCON

I tell you as my sister; you know what meaneth 'mum'!

              [*Exit* DAME CHAT]

[Act IV, Scene iv]

DICCON

Now lack I but my doctor to play his part again –
And lo where he cometh towards, peradventure to his
     pain!

              [*Enter* DOCTOR RAT]

DOCTOR RAT

What, good news, Diccon, fellow? Is Mother Chat at
     home?

DICCON

She is, sir, and she is not, but it please her to whom;
Yet did I take her tardy, as subtle as she was.   5

DOCTOR RAT

The thing that thou wentst for, hast thou brought it to
     pass?

DICCON

I have done that I have done, be it worse, be it better,
And Dame Chat at her wit's end I have almost set her.

DOCTOR RAT

Why, hast thou spied the nee'le? Quickly, I pray thee, tell!

DICCON

I have spied it, in faith, sir, I handled myself so well,   10

---

40 *He . . . water* Unless the meaning is only figurative, i.e., that Hodge will find himself in trouble ('in hot water'), this may support the identification of *lead* (l. 31)
as a cauldron or large vat; this receptacle, full of scalding water, would be sitting
in the fireplace where the thief would arrive after crawling through the hole behind or in the back of it (see l. 31n. above). Dame Chat plans a horrible recep-
tion for Hodge. The real intruder's eventual fate is less grim, as befits a comedy.

42 s.d. *Exit* DAME CHAT eds

Act IV, Scene iv See headnote to IV.iii.

  2 *towards* this way

  2 s.d. Enter DOCTOR RAT eds

  4 *She . . . whom* It depends on who wishes to see her

  5 *did . . . tardy* I caught her unawares

And yet the crafty quean had almost take my trump.
But or all came to an end, I set her in a dump.

DOCTOR RAT

How so, I pray thee, Diccon?

DICCON   Marry, sir will ye hear?
She was clapped down on the backside, by Cock's mother
    dear,
And there she sat sewing a halter or a band,   15
With no other thing save Gammer's needle in her hand.
As soon as any knock, if the filth be in doubt,
She needs but once puff, and her candle is out.
Now I, sir, knowing of every door the pin,
Came nicely, and said no word till time I was within;   20
And there I saw the nee'le, even with these two eyes.
Whoever say the contrary, I will swear he lies.

DOCTOR RAT

O Diccon, that I was not there then in thy stead!

DICCON

Well, if ye will be ordered and do by my rede,
I will bring you to a place, as the house stands,   25
Where ye shall take the drab with the nee'le in her hands.

DOCTOR RAT

For God's sake, do so, Diccon, and I will gage my gown,
To give thee a full pot of the best ale in the town.

DICCON

Follow me but a little and mark what I will say.
Lay down your gown beside you. Go to, come on your
    way.   30
See ye not what is here? A hole wherein ye may creep
Into the house, and suddenly unwares among them leap.
There shall ye find the bitchfox and the nee'le together.

11 *had ... trump* nearly found me out
12 *dump* gloomy mood
14 *Cock's* God's
20 *nicely* cautiously, quietly
27 *gage* pawn
29 *gown* The parson's costume would clearly announce his profession.
29–44 Ways in which this episode might have been staged are discussed in the
    Introduction. Q provides no stage directions whatsoever. It is at least clear that
    Rat is 'within' during ll. 39–44, and that Diccon speaks first to him (40–41),
    then to Dame Chat and, presumably, Doll (41–3), perhaps through the door of
    Chat's house. It is also clear that Diccon disappears before Rat reappears vow-
    ing vengeance; Diccon is then absent until V.ii.
32 *unwares* unexpectedly
33 *bitchfox* vixen

Do as I bid you, man; come on your ways hither!

DOCTOR RAT

Art thou sure, Diccon, the swill tub stands not
    hereabout?   35

DICCON

I was within myself, man, even now; there is no doubt.
Go softly, make no noise; give me your foot, Sir John.
Here will I wait upon you till you come out anon.

               [DOCTOR RAT *crawls into the hole*]

DOCTOR RAT [*Within*]

Help, Diccon! Out alas, I shall be slain among them!

DICCON

If they give you not the needle, tell them that ye will
    hang them.   40
'Ware that! – How, my wenches, have ye caught the fox
That used to make revel among your hens and cocks?
Save his life yet, for his order, though he sustain some
    pain. –
Gog's bread! I am afraid they will beat out his brain!

                          [*Exit*]

        [*Enter* DOCTOR RAT *from the hole*]

DOCTOR RAT

Woe worth the hour that I came here,   45
And woe worth him that wrought this gear!
A sort of drabs and queans have me blessed –
Was ever creature half so evil dressed?
Whoever it wrought and first did invent it,
He shall, I warrant him, ere long repent it.   50
I will spend all I have without my skin,
But he shall be brought to the plight I am in.
Master Bailey, I trow, and he be worth his ears,

---

35 *swill tub* tub for kitchen refuse, usually the slops (swill) fed to pigs
37 *Sir John* A familiar name for priests, often contemptuous of their ignorance, as
    in 'Sir John Lack-Latin'; compare 'Sir Oliver Martext' as *As You Like It*. 'Sir' in
    no way implies knighthood.
39 *Out alas* (exclamation of dismay)
41 *'Ware that* Be sure not to forget that; or, beware that blow
43 *for . . . order* because he is a clergyman
44 s.d. ed.
45 *Woe worth* Curse
47 *blessed* (ironic) beaten
48 *dressed* treated

Will snaffle these murderers and all that them bears.
I will surely neither bite nor sup   55
Till I fetch him hither, this matter to take up.   [*Exit*]

Act V, Scene i

[*Enter* MASTER BAILEY, SCAPETHRIFT *his servant, and* DOCTOR RAT]

MASTER BAILEY
  I can perceive none other, I speak it from my heart,
  But either ye are in all the fault, or else in the greatest
      part.
DOCTOR RAT
  If it be counted his fault, besides all his griefs,
  When a poor man is spoiled and beaten among thieves,
  Then I confess my fault herein, at this season.   5
  But I hope you will not judge so much against reason.
MASTER BAILEY
  And, methinks, by your own tale, of all that ye name,
  If any played the thief, you were the very same.
  The women, they did nothing, as your words make
      probation,
  But stoutly withstood your forcible invasion.   10
  If that a thief at your window to enter should begin,
  Would you hold forth your hand and help to pull him in,
  Or you would keep him out? I pray you, answer me.
DOCTOR RAT
  Marry, keep him out, and a good cause why!
  But I am no thief, sir, but an honest learned clerk.   15
MASTER BAILEY
  Yea, but who knoweth that when he meets you in the
      dark?

---

54 *snaffle* restrain   *all . . . bears* all who take their part

Act V, Scene i At least a brief lapse of dramatic time must be assumed here, while Rat
    goes in search of, finds and returns with Bailey, having told him his story mean-
    while. A song or musical interlude may have been performed, as between Acts I
    and II, and III and IV, though there is no evidence for it in the text.
  2 *ye . . . fault* the wrongdoing is entirely your own
  3 *griefs* ed. (grieves Q) injuries
  4 *spoiled* seriously injured
  5 *season* time
  9 *make probation* prove
  16–17, 22–4 Many proverbs express the same sentiment; John Heywood (1546)
    records 'As good is the foul as the fair in the dark'.

I am sure your learning shines not out at your nose!
Was it any marvel though the poor woman arose
And start up, being afraid of that was in her purse?
Methink you may be glad that your luck was no worse.   20
DOCTOR RAT
Is not this evil enough, I pray you, as you think?

Showing his broken head

MASTER BAILEY
Yea, but a man in the dark, if chances do wink,
As soon he smites his father as any other man,
Because for lack of light, discern him he ne can.
Might it not have been your luck with a spit to have been
          slain?   25
DOCTOR RAT
I think I am little better; my scalp is cloven to the brain!
If there be all the remedy, I know who bears the knocks.
MASTER BAILEY
By my troth, and well worthy, besides, to kiss the stocks.
To come in on the back side when ye might go about!
I know none such, unless they long to have their brains
          knocked out.   30
DOCTOR RAT
Well, will you be so good, sir, as talk with Dame Chat,
And know what she intended? I ask no more but that.
MASTER BAILEY [*To* SCAPETHRIFT]
Let her be called, fellow, because of Master Doctor.

[SCAPETHRIFT *knocks at* DAME CHAT'*s door*]

19 *of that* for that which
22 *if . . . wink* if he is unlucky
24 *ne can* cannot
27 *If . . . knocks* If that is all the comfort I can expect, I'm the one who has to suffer
28 *kiss . . . stocks* be confined in the stocks; a common form of public punishment for minor transgressions. This and that at V.ii.52 are the only recorded occurrences of the expression.
29 *To . . . about* Alludes to Rat's sneaking into Chat's house through the hole when he might have used the front door.
33 s.d. SCAPETHRIFT . . . *door* Tydeman (*goes to Dame Chat's house* Adams). As Adams and Tydeman realize, since both women's houses are on stage, Scapethrift need do no more than leave Bailey and Rat and go over to Chat's door, knock, and bring her back with him to them. Scapethrift's name is omitted from the list of characters at the head of V.ii; he was forgotten because he is mute, but he clearly has a function, that of going off in search of various characters as they are needed.

I warrant in this case she will be her own proctor;
She will tell her own tale in metre or in prose,   35
And bid you seek your remedy and so go wipe your
    nose.

Act V, Scene ii

[*Enter* DAME CHAT]

MASTER BAILEY
Dame Chat, Master Doctor upon you here complained,
That you and your maids should him much misorder,
And taketh many an oath that no word he feigned,
Laying to your charge how you thought him to murder;
And on his part again, that same man saith further,   5
He never offended you in word nor intent.
To hear you answer hereto, we have now for you sent.

DAME CHAT
That I would have murdered him? Fie on him, wretch,
And evil mought he thee for it, our Lord I beseech!
I will swear on all the books that opens and shuts   10
He feigneth this tale out of his own guts;
For this seven weeks with me I am sure he sat not down. –
Nay, ye have other minions, in the other end of the town,
Where ye were liker to catch such a blow,
Than anywhere else, as far as I know.   15

MASTER BAILEY
Belike then, Master Doctor, yon stripe there ye got
    not.

---

34 *proctor* attorney

0 s.d. *Enter . . .* CHAT eds. See above note to V.i.33 s.d.
2 Perhaps this line should be deleted. It disrupts the rhyme of ll. 1 and 3 and is
    superfluous since ll. 4 and 5 rhyme correctly. But as it stands, Bailey's speech is
    a rhyme royal stanza (*ababbcc*) in hexameters.
5 *further* ed. (furder Q)
9 *evil . . . thee* ill may he thrive (Boas)
12–15 Dame Chat implies that Doctor Rat spends most of his time at another ale-
    house at the other, in her opinion less respectable, end of town. He was found
    by Cock at Hob Filcher's house (III.iv.26); see gloss on *filching* (l. 53, below).
13 *minions* (contemptuous) creatures
16 *Belike* Likely

DOCTOR RAT

Think you I am so mad that where I was beat I wot not?
Will you believe this quean before she hath tried it?
It is not the first deed she hath done and afterward denied
it.

DAME CHAT

What, man, will you say I broke your head?

DOCTOR RAT   How canst
thou prove the contrary?   20

DAME CHAT

Nay, how provest thou that I did the deed?

DOCTOR RAT   Too plainly,
by St. Mary!
This proof I trow may serve, though I no word spoke!

[Showing his broken head]

DAME CHAT

Because thy head is broken, was it I that it broke?
I saw thee, Rat, I tell thee, not once within this fortnight.

DOCTOR RAT

No, marry, thou sawest me not, for why thou hadst no
light,   25
But I felt thee, for all the dark, beshrew thy smooth
cheeks!
And thou groped me, this will declare, any day this six
weeks.

Showing his head

MASTER BAILEY

Answer me to this, Master Rat: when caught you this
harm of yours?

DOCTOR RAT

A while ago, sir, God he knoweth, within less than these
two hours.

---

18 *tried* proved
25 *for why* because
26 *for ... dark* The alleged obscurity inside Chat's house is crucial: she still thinks
   that it was Hodge who sneaked in through the hole and was beaten by herself
   and her maid. Her error, and Rat's uncomprehending insistence, are maintained
   until ll. 180 ff.
   beshrew ... cheeks (a common oath.)
   beshrew curse
27 *And* If
   groped grasped, seized

MASTER BAILEY

    Dame Chat, was there none with you (confess i' faith)
        about that season?   30

    What, woman, let it be what it will, 'tis neither felony nor
        treason.

DAME CHAT

    Yes, by my faith, Master Bailey, there was a knave not
        far,

    Who caught one good fillip on the brow with a door bar,

    And well was he worthy, as it seemed to me.

    But what is that to this man, since this was not he?   35

MASTER BAILEY

    Who was it then? Let's hear.

DOCTOR RAT   Alas, sir, ask you that?

    Is it not made plain enough by the own mouth of Dame
        Chat?

    The time agreeth, my head is broken, her tongue cannot
        lie;

    Only upon a bare 'nay' she saith it was not I.

DAME CHAT

    No, marry, was it not, indeed, ye shall hear by this one
        thing: 40

    This afternoon a friend of mine for good will gave me
        warning,

    And bad me well look to my roost and all my capons'
        pens,

    For if I took not better heed, a knave would have my
        hens.

    Then I, to save my goods, took so much pains as him to watch,

    And as good fortune served me, it was my chance him
        for to catch.   45

    What strokes he bare away, or other what was his gains,

    I wot not, but sure I am he had something for his pains.

MASTER BAILEY

    Yet tells thou not who it was.

DAME CHAT   Who it was? A false thief,

    That came like a false fox, my pullen to kill and mischief!

MASTER BAILEY

    But knowest thou not his name?

DAME CHAT   I know it, but what
        then?   50

33 *fillip* blow
49 *pullen* ed. (pullaine Q) poultry
50 *what then* what of it

It was that crafty cullion Hodge, my Gammer Gurton's
  man.
MASTER BAILEY [*To* SCAPETHRIFT]
  Call me the knave hither; he shall sure kiss the stocks.
  I shall teach him a lesson for filching hens or cocks!

          [SCAPETHRIFT *knocks at* GAMMER GURTON'*s door*]

DOCTOR RAT
  I marvel, Master Bailey, so bleared be your eyes;
  An egg is not so full of meat as she is full of lies.   55
  When she hath played this prank, to excuse all this gear,
  She layeth the fault in such a one as I know was not there.
DAME CHAT
  Was he not there? Look on his pate, that shall be his
    witness!
DOCTOR RAT
  I would my head were half so whole; I would seek no
    redress!

          [*Enter* GAMMER GURTON]

MASTER BAILEY
  God bless you, Gammer Gurton.
GAMMER GURTON   God dild you, master
    mine.   60
MASTER BAILEY
  Thou hast a knave within thy house, Hodge, a servant of
    thine;
  They tell me that busy knave is such a filching one,
  That hen, pig, goose or capon thy neighbour can have
    none.
GAMMER GURTON
  By God, cham much amoved to hear any such report;
  Hodge was not wont, ich trow, to b'ave him in that
    sort.   65

---

51 *cullion* (Fr., couillon = testicle) rascal
53 *filching* stealing
53 s.d. SCAPETHRIFT . . . *door* Tydeman. Bailey's impatience at l. 78 and the author's
    gloss on ll. 80–1 make sense only if we assume that Scapethrift is encountering
    resistance from Hodge in his efforts to bring him out for interrogation.
59 *half so whole* (i.e., as Hodge's)
59 s.d. *Enter* GAMMER GURTON eds
60 *dild* eds. (dylde Q; corrupt form of 'yield') reward
64 *amoved* ed. (ameved Q; obsolete form) stirred, aroused
65 *wont* in the habit
    b'ave ed. (bave Q) behave

DAME CHAT

> A thievisher knave is not on live, more filching nor more
>   false;
> Many a truer man than he has hanged up by the halse.
> And thou, his dame, of all his theft thou art the sole
>   receiver;
> For Hodge to catch and thou to keep, I never knew none
>   better!

GAMMER GURTON [*To* MASTER BAILEY]

> Sir-reverence of your masterdom, and you were out
>   a-door,   70
> Chwould be so bold, for all her brags, to call her arrant
>   whore.
> [*To* DAME CHAT] And ich knew Hodge as bad as thou, ich
>   wish me endless sorrow
> And chould not take the pains to hang him up before
>   tomorrow!

DAME CHAT

> What have I stolen from thee or thine, thou ill-favoured
>   old trot?

GAMMER GURTON

> A great deal more, by God's blessed, than chever by thee
>   got!   75
> That thou knowest well; I need not say it.

MASTER BAILEY   Stop there, I
>   say,
> And tell me here, I pray you, this matter by the way:
> How chance Hodge is not here? Him would I fain have
>   had.

GAMMER GURTON

> Alas, sir, he'll be here anon; ha' be handled too bad.

DAME CHAT

> Master Bailey, sir, ye be not such a fool, well I know,   80
> But ye perceive by this lingering, there is a pad in the
>   straw.

---

66 *on live* living   67 *halse* neck
70 *Sir . . . a-door* With all respect to your worship, if you were not present
71 *Chwould* ed. (Chold Q)
72 *And . . . thou* If I knew that Hodge were as bad as you are
75 *chever* ich ever
79 *ha' be* ed. (ha be Q) he has been
81 *But ye* that you do not
    lingering delaying   *pad* toad
    a pad . . . straw Proverbial (Tilley P9). Usually a hidden danger; here, simply a
    cover-up.

Thinking that Hodge's head was broke, and that
Gammer would not let him come before them

GAMMER GURTON

Chill show you his face, ich warrant thee. Lo now, where
he is.

[*Enter* HODGE]

MASTER BAILEY

Come on, fellow. It is told me thou art a shrew, iwis:
Thy neighbour's hens thou takest, and plays the two-
legged fox;
Their chickens and their capons too, and now and then
their cocks.   85

HODGE

Ich defy them all that dare it say! Cham as true as the
best!

MASTER BAILEY

Wert not thou take within this hour, in Dame Chat's
hens' nest?

HODGE

Take there? No, master, chwould not do't, for a house
full of gold!

DAME CHAT

Thou or the devil in thy coat, swear this I dare be bold!

DOCTOR RAT

Swear me no swearing, quean, the devil he give thee
sorrow!   90
All is not worth a gnat thou canst swear till tomorrow.
Where is the harm he hath? Show it, by God's bread!
Ye beat him, with a witness, but the stripes light on my
head!

HODGE

Beat me? Gog's blessed body, could first, ich trow, have
burst thee!
Ich think, and chad my hands loose, callet, chwould have
crushed thee!   95

---

83 *shrew* rascal, villain
   iwis indeed
87, 88 *take* taken
88 *chwould* ed. (chold Q)
93 *with a witness* (ironically) without a doubt
94 *could* ed. (chold Q) I should
95 *chwould* ed. (chould Q)
   crushed ed. (crust Q)

DAME CHAT

Thou shitten knave, I trow thou knowest the full weight
of my fist!

I am foully deceived unless thy head and my door bar
kissed.

HODGE

Hold thy chat, whore! Thou criest so loud can no man
else be heard.

DAME CHAT

Well, knave, and I had thee alone, I would surely rap thy
costard!

MASTER BAILEY

Sir, answer me to this: is thy head whole or broken?   100

DAME CHAT

Yea, Master Bailey, blessed be every good token!

HODGE

Is my head whole? Ich warrant you, 'tis neither scurvy nor
scald.

What, you foul beast, does think 'tis either pilled or bald?

Nay, ich thank God! Chill not, for all that thou mayst
spend,

That chad one scab on my narse as broad as thy finger's
end.   105

MASTER BAILEY

Come nearer here.   HODGE   Yes, that ich dare.

MASTER BAILEY   By our lady, here is
no harm!

Hodge's head is whole enough, for all Dame Chat's
charm.

DAME CHAT

By Gog's blessed, however the thing he cloaks or
smoulders,

---

99 *costard* head

101 s.p. DAME CHAT Some editors give this line to Hodge, but the emendation is er-
roneous: Chat applauds Bailey's direct query to Hodge and 'blesses' the 'good
tokens' (i.e., the marks of the beating) she expects to see on his head. Bailey
refers to her blessing ('charm') in l. 107.

102 *scurvy* from *scurf*, an abnormal scaly condition of the scalp
    scald scabby

103 *pilled* shaven

105 *my narse* mine arse

108 *smoulders* smothers

I know the blows he bare away, either with head or
   shoulders.
Camest thou not, knave, within this hour, creeping into   110
   my pens,
And there was caught within my house, groping among
   my hens?

HODGE

A plague both on thy hens and thee! A cart, whore, a cart!
Chwould I were hanged as high as a tree, and chwere as
   false as thou art!
Give my Gammer again her washical thou stole away in
   thy lap.

GAMMER GURTON

Yea, Master Bailey, there is a thing you know not on,
   mayhap.   115
This drab, she keeps away my good, the devil he might
   her snare!
Ich pray you that ich might have a right action on her.

DAME CHAT

Have I thy good, old filth, or any such old sow's?
I am as true, I would thou knew, as skin between thy
   brows!

GAMMER GURTON

Many a truer hath been hanged, though you escape the   120
   danger.

DAME CHAT

Thou shalt answer, by God's pity, for this thy foul
   slander!

MASTER BAILEY [*To* GAMMER GURTON]

Why, what can ye charge her withal? To say so ye do not
   well.

GAMMER GURTON

Marry, a vengeance to her heart! That whore has stolen
   my nee'le!

DAME CHAT

Thy needle, old witch! How so? It were alms thy skull to
   knock!
So didst thou say the other day that I had stolen thy cock   125

---

112 *cart* See III.iii.23n.
114 *washical* what-do-you-call-it. The object is finally named at l. 123.
117 *a ... action* due process of law
119 *as true ... brows* Proverbial (Tilley S506). First recorded occurrrence.
124 *were alms* would be a good deed

And roasted him to my breakfast, which shall not be
    forgotten.
The devil pull out thy lying tongue and teeth that be so
    rotten!
GAMMER GURTON
Give me my nee'le! As for my cock, chwould be very
    loath
That chould hear tell he should hang on thy false faith
    and troth.
MASTER BAILEY
Your talk is such, I can scarce learn who should be most
    in fault.   130
GAMMER GURTON
Yet shall ye find no other wight save she, by bread and
    salt!
MASTER BAILEY
Keep ye content awhile; see that your tongues ye hold.
Methinks you should remember this is no place to scold.
How knowest thou, Gammer Gurton, Dame Chat thy
    needle had?
GAMMER GURTON
To name you, sir, the party, chould not be very glad.   135
MASTER BAILEY
Yea, but we must needs hear it, and therefore say it
    boldly.
GAMMER GURTON
Such one as told the tale, fully soberly and coldly,
Even he that looked on, will swear on a book,
What time this drunken gossip my fair long nee'le up
    took;
Diccon, master, the bedlam; cham very sure ye know
    him.   140
MASTER BAILEY
A false knave, by God's pity! Ye were but a fool to trow
    him.
I durst adventure well the price of my best cap

128 *chwould* ed. (chould Q)
128-9 *As ... troth* I would not like to be told that my cock's fate was dependent on
    your false oaths.
129 *chould* ed. (chuld Q) I should
131 *wight* person
    by ... salt (oath)
141 *trow* believe
142 *adventure* wager

That when the end is known, all will turn to a jape.
[*To* GAMMER GURTON] Told he not you that, besides, she
    stole your cock that tide?
GAMMER GURTON
No, master, no indeed, for then he should have lied;   145
My cock is, I thank Christ, safe and well a-fine.
DAME CHAT
Yea, but that ragged colt, that whore, that Tib of thine,
Said plainly thy cock was stolen and in my house was
    eaten.
That lying cut is lost, that she is not swinged and beaten;
And yet, for all my good name, it were a small amends.   150
I pick not this gear, hearst thou, out of my fingers' ends,
But he that heard it told me, who thou of late didst name:
Diccon, whom all men knows – it was the very same.
MASTER BAILEY [*To* GAMMER GURTON]
This is the case: you lost your needle about the doors,
And she answers again, she has no cock of yours.   155
Thus in your talk and action, from that you do intend,
She is whole five mile wide, from that she doth defend.
Will you say she hath your cock?
GAMMER GURTON   No marry, sir, that chill
    not.
MASTER BAILEY [*To* DAME CHAT]
Will you confess her needle?
DAME CHAT   Will I? No sir, will I not!
MASTER BAILEY
Then, there lieth all the matter.
GAMMER GURTON   Soft, master, by the way;   160
Ye know she could do little and she could not say nay!
MASTER BAILEY
Yea, but he that made one lie about your cock stealing
Will not stick to make another, what time lies be in
    dealing.

143 *jape* jest
144 *that tide* at that time
146 *a-fine* in the end
149 *cut* See III.iii.25 n.
    lost damned
    that . . . not if she is not
149–50 *That . . . amends* The slut deserves to be soundly thrashed, but even that
    would hardly compensate for my tarnished reputation.
161 *Ye . . . nay* it's easy enough for her to say 'no'
163 *stick* hesitate
    what . . . dealing when lies are so current

I ween the end will prove this brawl did first arise
Upon no other ground but only Diccon's lies.   165
DAME CHAT
Though some be lies, as you belike have espied them,
Yet other some be true; by proof I have well tried them.
MASTER BAILEY
What other thing beside this, Dame Chat?
DAME CHAT   Marry sir,
    even this:
The tale I told before, the selfsame tale it was his.
He gave me, like a friend, warning against my loss,   170
Else had my hens be stolen each one, by God's cross!
He told me Hodge would come, and in he came indeed,
But as the matter chanced, with greater haste than speed.
This truth was said and true was found, as truly I report.
MASTER BAILEY
If Doctor Rat be not deceived, it was of another sort.   175
DOCTOR RAT [*To* DAME CHAT]
By God's mother, thou and he be a couple of subtle
    foxes!
Between you and Hodge, I bear away the boxes.
Did not Diccon appoint the place where thou shouldst
    stand to meet him?
DAME CHAT
Yes, by the mass, and if he came, bad me not stick to spit
    him.
DOCTOR RAT
God's sacrament! The villain knave hath dressed us
    round about!   180
He is the cause of all this brawl, that dirty shitten lout!
When Gammer Gurton here complained, and made a
    rueful moan,
I heard him swear that you had gotten her needle that was
    gone.

166 *belike* in all likelihood
167 *other some* some others
173 *speed* success
      with . . . speed Proverbial (Tilley H197): 'More haste than good speed'.
177 *boxes* blows
179 *spit* ed. (speet Q) stab
180 *dressed . . . about* played dirty tricks on all of us
182 *rueful* pitiful
183–9 Doctor Rat is recalling IV.iv.10–34. Diccon had previously refused to swear
      (IV.ii.39–49).

And this to try, he further said he was full loath; howbeit,
He was content with small ado to bring me where to see
    it.   185
And where ye sat, he said full certain, if I would follow his
    rede,
Into your house a privy way he would me guide and lead,
And where ye had it in your hands, sewing about a clout
And set me in the back hole, thereby to find you out.
And whiles I sought a quietness, creeping upon my
    knees,   190
I found the weight of your door bar for my reward and
    fees!
Such is the luck that some men gets, while they begin to
    mell
In setting at one such as were out, minding to make all
    well.

HODGE

Was not well blessed, Gammer, to 'scape that scour? And
    chad been there,
Then chad been dressed, belike, as ill, by the mass, as
    Gaffer Vicar.   195

MASTER BAILEY

Marry, sir, here is a sport alone; I looked for such an end.
If Diccon had not played the knave, this had been soon
    amend.
My Gammer here he made a fool, and dressed her as she
    was,
And Goodwife Chat he set to school, till both parts cried
    'Alas!'
And Doctor Rat was not behind, whiles Chat his crown
    did pare;   200
I would the knave had been stark blind, if Hodge had not
    his share.

HODGE

Cham meetly well sped already amongs, cham dressed
    like a colt!

---

184 *try* prove   *loath; howbeit,* eds (loth how be it Q)
188 *clout* cloth
192 *mell* interfere
193 *in . . . out* trying to reconcile those who were at odds
194 *scour* attack
197 *amend* amended
199 *set to school* gave her a lesson   *parts* parties
202 *amongs* all this while   *dressed* served, treated

And chad not had the better wit, chad been made a dolt.

MASTER BAILEY [*To* SCAPETHRIFT]

Sir knave, make haste Diccon were here! Fetch him
wherever he be!

[*Exit* SCAPETHRIFT]

DAME CHAT

Fie on the villain, fie, fie, that makes us thus agree!   205

GAMMER GURTON

Fie on him, knave, with all my heart, now fie and fie
again!

DOCTOR RAT

'Now fie on him!' may I best say, whom he hath almost
slain.

[*Enter* SCAPETHRIFT *and* DICCON]

MASTER BAILEY

Lo, where he cometh at hand! Belike he was not far.

Diccon, here be two or three thy company cannot spare.

DICCON

God bless you, and you may be blessed, so many all at
once.   210

DAME CHAT

Come, knave, it were a good deed to geld thee, by Cock's
bones!

Seest not thy handiwork? Sir Rat, can ye forbear him?

[DOCTOR RAT *strikes* DICCON]

---

204 s.d. *Exit* SCAPETHRIFT eds
205 *agree* disagree
210 *and* if
211 *geld* castrate
   Cock's God's
212 *forbear him* restrain yourself from punishing him
   s.d. DOCTOR … DICCON Baskervill *et al.* Doctor Rat is egged on by Dame Chat,
   and Diccon's lines (213–15) make no sense if Rat has not done something; it is
   obvious that he has done something with his hands, since Diccon curses them
   specifically.

DICCON

A vengeance on those hands light, for my hands came not
near him!
The whoreson priest hath lift the pot in some of these
alewives' chairs,
That his head would not serve him, belike, to come down
the stairs.   215

MASTER BAILEY

Nay, soft, thou mayst not play the knave and have this
language too;
If thou thy tongue bridle awhile, the better mayst thou
do.
Confess the truth as I shall ask and cease a while to fable,
And for thy fault I promise thee thy handling shall be
reasonable.
Hast thou not made a lie or two, to set these two by the
ears?   220

DICCON

What if I have? Five hundred such have I seen within
these seven years.
I am sorry for nothing else but that I see not the sport
Which was between them when they met, as they
themselves report.

MASTER BAILEY

The greatest thing – Master Rat – ye see how he is
dressed?

DICCON

What devil need he be groping so deep in Goodwife
Chat's hens' nest?   225

MASTER BAILEY

Yea, but it was thy drift to bring him into the briars.

DICCON

God's bread! Hath not such an old fool wit to save his
ears!

214 *lift* lifted
214–15 *The whoreson ... stairs* He was so drunk that he fell downstairs. This is
    Diccon's 'explanation' for Rat's wounded head. He pretends to think he is being
    accused of actually beating Rat himself.
218 *fable* speak falsely
221 *within ... years* Not intended as a precise length of time; vague, as is 'five hun-
    dred such'.
222 *see* saw
226 *drift* plot, design
    bring ... briars Proverbial (Tilley B673): 'To leave in the briars'.
    briars trouble

He showeth himself herein, ye see, so very a cox,
The cat was not so madly allured by the fox
To run into the snares was set for him, doubtless,   230
For he leapt in for mice, and this Sir John for madness!

DOCTOR RAT

Well, and ye shift no better, ye losel, lither and lazy,
I will go near for this to make ye leap at a daisy.
In the king's name, Master Bailey, I charge you set him
    fast.

DICCON

What, fast at cards or fast on sleep? It is the thing I did
    last.   235

DOCTOR RAT

Nay, fast in fetters, false varlet, according to thy deeds!

MASTER BAILEY

Master Doctor, there is no remedy, I must entreat you
    needs
Some other kind of punishment –

DOCTOR RAT   Nay, by all hallows!
His punishment, if I may judge, shall be naught else but
    the gallows!

MASTER BAILEY

That were too sore! A spiritual man to be so extreme!   240

DOCTOR RAT

Is he worthy any better, sir? How do ye judge and deem?

MASTER BAILEY

I grant him worthy punishment, but in no wise so great.

---

228 *cox* eds (coxe [= cokes] Q) fool, one easily 'taken in'. To rhyme with 'fox', obviously.
   Compare the name 'Bartholmew Cokes', the ninny in Jonson's *Bartholmew Fair*.

229–31 *The cat ... madness* Diccon refers to a story from the popular *History of
   Reynard the Fox* (and not Aesop's fables, in one of which it is the fox who is the
   victim of his own folly while the cat saves himself), translated by William
   Caxton in 1481 and reprinted several times before 1550. See Appendix for a full
   text. Ironically, Diccon had alluded to fox and hens at IV.iv.41–2, and then recalls the Reynard story explicitly here, when it is he himself who has played the
   fox's role. Dame Chat has made the same comparison at l. 49 and Bailey at l.
   84.

232 *losel* scoundrel, ne'er-do-well
   lither good-for-nothing

233 *will go near* am on the point of
   leap ... daisy Proverbial (Tilley D14). To be hanged. Occurs also in Udall's
   Respublica (1553).

234 *In ... name* See Introduction, p. xiii.

235 *on sleep* asleep   236 *varlet* knave

237 *needs* necessarily   238 *all hallows* all the saints

GAMMER GURTON

It is a shame, ich tell you plain, for such false knaves
    entreat!
He has almost undone us all – that is as true as steel –
And yet for all this great ado, cham never the near my
    nee'le!   245

MASTER BAILEY

Canst thou not say anything to that, Diccon, with least or
    most?

DICCON

Yea marry, sir, thus much I can say well: the needle is lost.

MASTER BAILEY

Nay, canst not thou tell which way that needle may be
    found?

DICCON

No, by my fay, sir, though I might have an hundred
    pound.

HODGE

Thou liar, lickdish, didst not say the nee'le would be
    gitten?   250

DICCON

No, Hodge, by the same token, you were that time
    beshitten
For fear of Hobgobling – you wot well what I mean;
As long as it is since, I fear me yet ye be scarce clean.

MASTER BAILEY

Well, Master Rat, you must both learn and teach us to
    forgive.

244 *as true as steel* Proverbial (Tilley S840).
245 *never the near* no nearer
246 *with ... most* at all
249 *fay* faith
250 *lickdish* parasite *gitten* gotten
252 *Hobgobling* Hobgoblin, another name for Puck or Robin Goodfellow, but also any mischievous or evil spirit, a bogeyman. Diccon refers to the devil he was conjuring in II.i.
254–61 The particulars of Bailey's proposition are not entirely clear, but he seems to be saying to Rat: since Diccon has confessed, I will impose a public penance on him, if you will drop your charges against him. In exchange for that, and in view of the injuries you have suffered, I am willing to cancel the charge against you (i.e. for illegally entering Dame Chat's house) though it will cost me the fee of twenty pence I would get for bringing you to justice. You may go free, if you agree to let the matter 'end with mirth'.

Since Diccon hath confession made and is so clean
    shrive,   255
If you to me consent, to amend this heavy chance,
I will enjoin him here some open kind of penance.
Of this condition (where ye know my fee is twenty pence)
For the bloodshed, I am agreed with you here to
    dispense;
Ye shall go quit, so that ye grant the matter now to run,   260
To end with mirth among us all, even as it was begun.

DAME CHAT

Say 'yea', Master Vicar, and he shall sure confess to be
    your debtor,
And all we that be here present will love you much the
    better.

DOCTOR RAT

My part is the worst, but since you all hereon agree,
Go even to, Master Bailey! Let it be so for me.   265

MASTER BAILEY

How sayest thou, Diccon? Art content this shall on me depend?

DICCON

Go to, Master Bailey, say on your mind. I know ye are my
    friend.

MASTER BAILEY

Then mark ye well: to recompense this thy former action,
Because thou hast offended all, to make them satisfaction,
Before their faces here kneel down, and as I shall thee
    teach,   270
So thou shalt take an oath of Hodge's leather breech:
First, for Master Doctor, upon pain of his curse,
Where he will pay for all, thou never draw thy purse;
And when ye meet at one pot, he shall have the first pull,
And thou shalt never offer him the cup but it be full.   275
To Goodwife Chat thou shalt be sworn, even on the same
    wise,
If she refuse thy money once, never to offer it twice;
Thou shalt be bound by the same here, as thou dost take
    it,

---

255 *clean shrive* (past participle) Completely absolved, freed from the consequences
    of sin or crime. Technically, and as used here, the step between confession and
    penance, but often used as including confession as well.
259 *dispense* (legal term) to remit the penalty of the law in a particular case
265 *Go even to* have done with you, be content
    for me for my part
270–1 *teach,/So thou* ed. (teach./For thou Q)

When thou mayst drink of free cost, thou never forsake it.
For Gammer Gurton's sake, again sworn shalt thou be,   280
To help her to her needle again if it do lie in thee;
And likewise be bound, by the virtue of that,
To be of good abearing to Gib her great cat.
Last of all for Hodge, the oath to scan,
Thou shalt never take him for fine gentleman.   285
HODGE
Come on, fellow Diccon, chall be even with thee now!
MASTER BAILEY
Thou wilt not stick to do this, Diccon, I trow.
DICCON
No, by my father's skin! My hand, down I lay it,
Look, as I have promised; I will not denay it.
But Hodge, take good heed now thou do not beshite me!   290

And gave him a good blow on the buttock

HODGE
Gog's heart, thou false villain, dost thou bite me?
MASTER BAILEY
What, Hodge, doth he hurt thee or ever he begin?
HODGE
He thrust me into the buttock with a bodkin or a pin!
I say, Gammer! Gammer!
GAMMER GURTON   How now, Hodge, how now?
HODGE
God's malt, Gammer Gurton!
GAMMER GURTON   Thou art mad, ich trow!   295
HODGE
Will you see the devil Gammer?
GAMMER GURTON   The devil, son? God bless
          us!
HODGE
Chwould ich were hanged, Gammer!
GAMMER GURTON   Marry, see, ye
          might dress us –
HODGE
Chave it, by the mass, Gammer!

281 *do . . . thee* is in your power
282 *that* (i.e., that same oath)
283 *good abearing* (legal phrase which passed into popular usage) good behaviour
284 *scan* recite briefly, sum up
289 *denay* deny
292 *or ever* even before
293 *bodkin* dagger or hairpin

GAMMER GURTON   What? Not my nee'le,
    Hodge!
HODGE
    Your nee'le, Gammer, your nee'le!
GAMMER GURTON   No, fie, dost but
    dodge!
HODGE
    Cha' found your nee'le, Gammer – here in my hand be it!   300
GAMMER GURTON
    For all the loves on earth, Hodge, let me see it!
HODGE
    Soft, Gammer.
GAMMER GURTON Good Hodge –
HODGE   Soft, ich say, tarry a while.
GAMMER GURTON
    Nay, sweet Hodge, say truth, and do not me beguile.
HODGE
    Cham sure on it, ich warrant you; it goes no more astray.
GAMMER GURTON
    Hodge, when I speak so fair, wilt still say me nay?   305
HODGE
    Go near the light, Gammer. This – well, in faith, good
        luck!
    Chwas almost undone, 'twas so far in my buttock!
GAMMER GURTON
    'Tis mine own dear nee'le, Hodge, sickerly I wot!
HODGE
    Am I not a good son, Gammer, am I not?
GAMMER GURTON
    Christ's blessing light on thee! Hast made me forever!   310
HODGE
    Ich knew that ich must find it, else chould a' had it never!
DAME CHAT
    By my troth, Gossip Gurton, I am even as glad
    As though I mine own self as good a turn had!
MASTER BAILEY
    And I, by my conscience, to see it so come forth,
    Rejoice so much at it as three needles be worth!   315
DOCTOR RAT
    I am no whit sorry to see you so rejoice.

---

299 *dodge* prevaricate   308 *sickerly* without doubt
309 *Am I … am I* ed. (Cham I … cham I Q; the 'ch-' form is redundant here)
311 *chould* eds (choud Q) I should
316 *no whit* not at all

DICCON

    No I much the gladder for all this noise.

    Yet say 'Gramercy, Diccon', for springing of the game.

GAMMER GURTON

    Gramercy, Diccon, twenty times! O how glad cham!

    If that chould do so much – your masterdom to come

        hither,   320

    Master Rat, Goodwife Chat and Diccon together –

    Cha' but one halfpenny, as far as ich know it,

    And chill not rest this night till ich bestow it.

    If ever ye love me, let us go in and drink.

MASTER BAILEY

    I am content, if the rest think as I think.   325

    Master Rat, it shall be best for you if we so do;

    Then shall you warm you and dress yourself too.

DICCON

    Soft, sirs, take us with you – the company shall be the

        more;

    As proud comes behind, they say, as any goes before.

    [*To the audience*] But now, my good masters, since we

        must be gone,   330

    And leave you behind us, here all alone,

    Since at our last ending, thus merry we be,

    For Gammer Gurton's needle's sake, let us have a *plaudite!*

                                 [*Exeunt*]

Finis, Gurton. Perused and allowed, etc.
Imprinted at London
in Fleet Street beneath the Conduit,
at the sign of St. John Evangelist,
by
Thomas Colwell.
1575.

318 *springing . . . game* (from hunting) flushing the quarry from its hiding place

320 *chould* I could   *your masterdom* (i.e. Bailey)

327 *dress* take care of

329 *As . . . before* Proverbial (Tilley C536). Diccon acknowledges, somewhat sarcastically, the superior social status of the bailiff and the priest.

328–9 The lines are addressed to Bailey and Rat, who perhaps set off together. In production, the characters might begin filing into Dame Chat's alehouse (l. 324: 'let us go in and drink'), while Diccon speaks the last four lines to the audience.

333 *let . . . plaudite* This appeal for applause echoes the last line of the Prologue.

333 s.d. *Exeunt* eds (*They all go into the alehouse* Tydeman)

APPENDIX

From *The History of Reynard the Fox*, Chapter 10, translated from Dutch by William Caxton, 1481. The text is from N. F. Blake's edition for the Early English Text Society (1970), pp. 19–23, with spelling and punctuation modernized. The episode is a likely source for that in *Gammer Gurton's Needle*, IV.iv, in which Doctor Rat is led into a trap by the wily Diccon.

(Bruin the bear having been duped by Reynard and failed in his mission to bring him to court to answer grave charges brought against him by several of the animals, the cat Tibert is nominated by the king and his council to go in search of the wily fox).

Then the king said, 'Sir Tibert, ye shall now go to Reynard and say to him this second time that he come to court unto the plea for to answer, for though he be fell to other beasts, he trusteth you well and shall do by your counsel. And tell if he come not, he shall have the third warning and be dayed, and if he then come not, we shall proceed by right against him and all his lineage without mercy'.

Tibert spake, 'My lord the king, they that this counselled you were not my friends. What shall I do there? He will not for me neither come nor abide. I beseech you, dear king, send some other to him. I am little and feeble. Bruin the bear which was so great and strong could not bring him. How should I then take it on hand?'

'Nay', said the king, 'Sir Tibert, ye been wise and well learned. Though ye be not great, there lieth not on. Many do more with craft and cunning than with might and strength'.

'Then', said the cat, 'sith it must needs be done, I must then take it upon me. God give grace that I may well achieve it, for my heart is heavy and evil willed thereto'. Tibert made him soon ready toward Maleperduis ... There he found the fox alone standing tofore his house.

Tibert said, 'The rich God give you good even, Reynard. The king hath menaced you for to take your life from you if ye come not now with me to the court'.

The fox tho spake and said, 'Tibert, my dear cousin, ye be right welcome. I would well truly that ye had much good luck'. (What hurted the fox to speak fair; though he said well, his heart thought it not, and that shall be seen ere they depart).

fell cruel, savage
dayed summoned to appear on a certain day
there lieth not on that is irrelevant, take no account of it
sith since   *even* evening
Maleperduis Reynard's castle   *tho* then
tofore before   *What* Which

Reynard said, 'Will we this night be together. I will make you good cheer, and tomorrow early in the dawning we will together go to the court. Good neve, let us so do. I have none of my kin that I trust so much to as to you. Here was Bruin the bear, the traitor: he looked so shrewdly on me and methought he was so strong that I would not for a thousand mark have gone with him. But cousin, I will tomorrow early go with you'.

Tibert said, 'It is best that we now go, for the moon shineth also light as it were day. I never saw fairer weather'.

'Nay, dear cousin, such might meet us by day time that would make us good cheer, and by night per adventure might do us harm. It is suspicious to walk by night. Therefore abide this night here by me'.

Tibert said, 'What should we eat if we abode here?'

Reynard said, 'Here is but little to eat. Ye may well have an honeycomb, good and sweet. What say ye, Tibert, will ye any thereof?'

Tibert answered, 'I set nought thereby. Have ye nothing else? If ye gave me a good fat mouse, I should be better pleased'.

'A fat mouse?' said Reynard, 'Dear cousin, what say ye? Hereby dwelleth a priest and hath a barn by his house. Therein been so many mice that a man should not lead them away upon a wain. I have heard the priest many times complain that they did him much harm'.

'O dear Reynard, lead me thither, for all that I may do for you'.

'Yea, Tibert, say ye me truth? Love ye well mice?'

'If I love them well!' said the cat. 'I love mice better than anything that men give me. Know ye not that mice savour better than venison, yea, than flans or pasties. Will ye well do? So lead me thither where the mice been and then shall ye win my love, yea, all had ye slain my father, mother, and all my kin'.

Reynard said, 'Ye mock and jape therewith'.

The cat said, 'So help me God, I do not!'

'Tibert', said the fox, 'wist I that verily, I would yet this night make that ye should be full of mice'.

'Reynard', quoth he, 'full? That were many!'

'Tibert, ye jape'.

'Reynard', quoth he, 'in truth I do not. If I had a fat mouse, I would not give it for a golden noble'.

neve nephew	*noble* coin
also as	*mark* marks (unit of money)
all had ye even if you had	*wain* wagon
wist . . . should if I really knew that (you were serious), I would ensure that tonight you should	*jape* joke

'Tibert', quoth the fox, 'I will bring you to the place ere I go from you'.

'Reynard', quoth the cat, 'upon your safe-conduct I would well go with you to Montpellier!'

'Let us then go', said the fox, 'we tarry all too long'.

Thus went they forth without letting to the place where as they would be, to the priest's barn, which was fast walled about with a mud wall. And the night tofore the fox had broken in and had stolen from the priest a good fat hen, and the priest, all angry, had set a grin tofore the hole to avenge him, for he would fain have take the fox. This knew well the fell thief the fox. And said, 'Sir Tibert, cousin, creep into this hole and ye shall not long tarry but that ye shall catch mice by great heaps. Hark how they peep! When ye be full, come again. I will tarry here after you before this hole. We will tomorrow go together to the court. Tibert, why tarry ye thus long? Come off, and so may we return soon to my wife which waiteth after us and shall make us good cheer'.

Tibert said, 'Reynard, cousin, is it then your counsel that I go into this hole? These priests been so wily and shrewish, I dread to take harm'.

'O ho, Tibert', said the fox, 'I saw you never so sore afeared. What aileth you?'

The cat was ashamed and sprang into the hole. And anon he was caught in the grin by the neck ere he wist. Thus deceived Reynard his guest and cousin.

As Tibert was ware of the grin, he was afeared and sprang forth. The grin went to. Then began he to wrawen, for he was almost y-strangled. He called, he cried and made a shrewd noise. Reynard stood tofore the hole and heard all and was well a-paid, and said, 'Tibert, love ye well mice? Be they fat and good? Knew the priest hereof or Martinet, they be so gentle that they would bring you sauce. Tibert, ye sing and eat. Is that the guise of the court? Lord God, if Ysegrim were there by you in such a rest as ye now be, then should I be glad, for oft he hath done me scathe and harm'.

---

upon . . . Montpellier under your protection, I would go anywhere (Montpellier being in the far south of France, presumably far from where the story is imagined to take place)
grin snare made with a string and a noose, which tightens about the victim's neck the more he struggles to escape
went to closed, tightened

a-paid satisfied
Ysegrim the wolf, the fox's main adversary in the *Reynard* cycles
scathe injury
letting hindrance
wist knew
wrawen cry out, screech

Tibert could not go away, be he mewed and galped so loud that Martinet sprang up and cried loud, 'God be thanked! My grin hath taken the thief that hath stolen our hens. Arise up! We will reward him'.

With these words arose the priest in an evil time and waked all them that were in the house, and cried with a loud voice 'The fox is take!' There leap and ran all that there was. The priest himself ran all mother-naked. Martinet was the first that came to Tibert. The priest took to Locken his wife an offering candle and bade her light it at fire, and he smote Tibert with a great staff. There received Tibert many a great stroke over all his body. Martinet was so angry that he smote the cat an eye out. The naked priest lift up and should have given a great stroke to Tibert but Tibert, that saw he must die, sprang between the priest's legs with his claws and with his teeth, that he raught out his right cullion or bollock-stone. That leap became ill to the priest and to his great shame. This thing fell down upon the floor. When Dame Julock knew that, she sware by her father's soul that she would it had cost her all the offering of a whole year that the priest had not had that harm, hurt and shame, and that it had not happed, and said in the devil's name was the grin there set. ...

The fox stood without tofore the hole and heard all these words and laughed so sore that he unneth could stand. ... When Tibert the cat saw them all busy about the priest, tho he began to bite and gnaw the grin in the middle asunder and sprang out of the hole, and went rolling and wentling towards the king's court.

Martinet the priest's son
galped yelped, bellowed
in ... time in (what proves to be for him) an unfortunate hour
that there was who were there
Locken Julock, the priest's wife
offering candle large votive candle from the church
cullion (Fr., *couillon*), *bollock-stone* testicle
unneth hardly
wentling stumbling

CPSIA information can be obtained
at www.ICGtesting.com
Printed in the USA
LVOW13s2350080817
544266LV00014BA/159/P